Mark Sarnecki

HARMONY

2nd Edition

FREDERICK
HARRIS
MUSIC

PREFACE

Harmony: Basic is designed to be a first-year harmony course. It approaches the study of harmony with an additive process. It begins with the basic progression V–I, and gradually expands the student's harmonic vocabulary. The student progresses from very simple harmonic progressions at the beginning, to more elaborate and complex progressions throughout. Each lesson presents a new idea with numerous exercises to reinforce the student's knowledge of the material being presented.

This book uses basic voice-leading rules to avoid a large number of exceptions, and exceptions to exceptions, which can be confusing to beginning harmony students. This has been done without compromising the musical integrity of the examples and exercises.

Teachers may wish to present other voice-leading options as they see fit. Melody writing, music analysis, and form are covered with carefully selected musical examples and exercises. Summaries are presented at strategic points throughout the book to help students review concepts already studied. This book is designed to teach Basic Harmony, but is effective as a general course of music study for harmony and voice-leading.

Mark Sarnecki

ACKNOWLEDGEMENTS

The author would like to thank the following people for their assistance in preparing this publication.

Editor: Kathleen Wood

Cover Art: Bruno Enderlin

Contents

LESSON 1
TONALITY, CHORD QUALITY, AND CHORD SYMBOLS

Music that is based on a major or minor scale is considered **tonal music.** In tonal music, one tone or note has greater importance or emphasis than the other notes of the scale. In fact, there is a hierarchy of pitches, with the tonic or key note being the most important note of the scale. When one single tone takes predominance it is called the **tonal center.**

Music based on the F major scale is said to be in the **key** of F major. F, the tonic, is the tonal center, and the music is in the **tonality** of F major. The terms "tonality" and "key" can often be used interchangeably.

A harmonic interval occurs when two notes sound simultaneously. These two notes may imply a specific chord, but generally two notes do not constitute a chord. At least three notes are required to make a complete chord. A three-note chord is called a **triad.**

The four qualities of **triads** that can be found in major and minor keys are:

major, minor, diminished, and augmented

 A **major triad** consists of the intervals of a major 3rd and perfect 5th above the root.

 A **minor triad** consists of the intervals of a minor 3rd and perfect 5th above the root.

 A **diminished triad** consists of the intervals of a minor 3rd and diminished 5th above the root.

 An **augmented triad** consists of the intervals of a major 3rd and augmented 5th above the root.

We can build a triad on each degree of the major and minor scales. These are the triads that occur on the notes of the major scale.

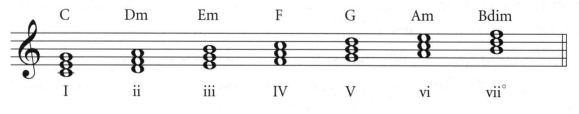

These are the triads that occur on the notes of the minor scale. Triads in minor keys are based on all three forms of the minor scale: natural, harmonic, and melodic.

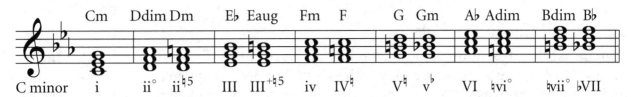

A **7th chord** is a four-note chord that is formed by adding the interval of a 3rd to a triad. This 3rd is placed above the fifth of the triad and becomes the seventh of the chord. The notes of this chord are referred to as the root, third, fifth and seventh.

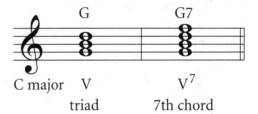

Just as there are different qualities of triads, there are different qualities of 7th chords. Each 7th chord has two parts to its name. The first part refers to the type of triad formed by the root, third, and fifth of the chord. The second refers to the interval quality of 7th formed between the root and the seventh of the chord.

The structural type of a dominant 7th is *major-minor*. Here, major refers to the triad and minor refers to the interval between the root and seventh. G–B–D is a major triad, and G to F is a minor 7th. V^7 often replaces V in a harmonic progression and is the most frequently used of all the 7th chords.

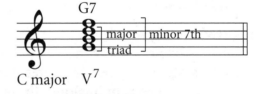

If both the triad and the 7th have the same name, for instance *major-major, minor-minor,* or *diminished-diminished*, the name is shortened to *major 7th, minor 7th,* or *diminished 7th*. Study these examples noting the type of triad and the interval between the root and the seventh.

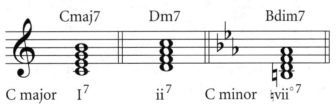

A diminished triad with a minor 7th, a *diminished-minor 7th*, is more commonly known as a *half-diminished 7th* chord. Every diatonic scale degree produces a specific quality of seventh chord. For example, the major-minor 7th chord only occurs on $\hat{5}$ in major and (harmonic) minor keys. The diminished 7th chord only occurs on the raised $\hat{7}$ in minor keys. A half-diminished 7th chord occurs on $\hat{7}$ of major keys and $\hat{2}$ in (harmonic) minor keys.

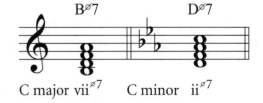

Chord Symbols

This book uses three different types of chords symbols.

Functional Chord Symbols

Functional chord symbols are Roman numerals placed below the staff; they identify the root of the chord by the scale degree on which it is built. Capital (uppercase) letters are used for major triads; lowercase letters are used for minor triads. A small circle (°) after a lowercase Roman numeral indicates a diminished triad. Seventh chords use the same Roman numeral as the triad, plus the number 7 placed at the upper right-hand corner. The diminished 7th chord is indicated by °7 and the half-diminished 7th chord is indicated by ⌀7.

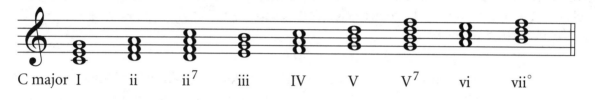

C major   I   ii   ii⁷   iii   IV   V   V⁷   vi   vii°

Figured Bass

Figured bass symbols specify a chord by its intervallic structure. Alone, they do not name the root of the chord or identify its quality. This is a system of indicating notes above the bass (the lowest part). When a triad is in **root position,** the intervals of a 5th and 3rd occur above the bass (C–G = 5th, C–E = 3rd). These intervals could be indicated by the numbers 5 and 3 below the chord.

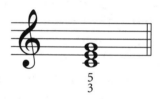

In normal figured bass notation, however, the notes of a triad in root position—the notes a 3rd and a 5th above the bass note—are understood. In other words, a triad in root position with no altered notes needs no figuration.

Figures are required, however, to indicate an altered 3rd or 5th above the root. An accidental without a number always refers to the 3rd above the bass note. If the fifth is altered, the accidental appears beside the number "5."

Study these chords built on notes of the minor scale.

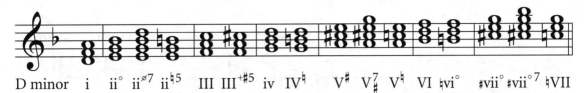

D minor   i   ii°   ii°⁷   ii♮5   III   III⁺♯5   iv   IV♮   V♯   V⁷♯   V♮   VI   ♭vi°   ♯vii°   ♯vii°⁷   ♭VII

An accidental without a number after the Roman numeral in the figuration always indicates the altered third. An accidental placed before a Roman numeral (for example, ♯vii°) indicates that the root is altered. An augmented triad is indicated by an uppercase Roman numeral and a plus sign (+)—for example, III⁺.

Root/Quality Chord Symbols

Root/quality chord symbols identify the root of the chord by its letter name and state the quality of the chord (major, minor, augmented, diminished). They do not indicate the key or the function of the chord within the key.

Study the following chords built on the C major scale. These chords are labeled with both functional and root/quality chord symbols.

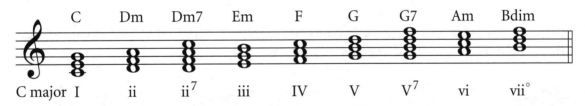

C major   I   ii   ii⁷   iii   IV   V   V⁷   vi   vii°

With root/quality chord symbols, major chords are represented by the root name alone. In C major, the I chord is a C major chord. Its root/quality chord symbol is C. ii is a D minor chord and is symbolized Dm. ii⁷ is a minor triad with a minor 7th and is symbolized Dm7. V⁷, the dominant 7th, is a major triad with a minor 7th and is symbolized G7. vii° is a diminished chord and is symbolized Bdim (an alternate root/quality symbol for this chord is B°).

1. For the following chords, name the key, write the functional chord symbols below the staff, and the root/quality chord symbols above the staff.

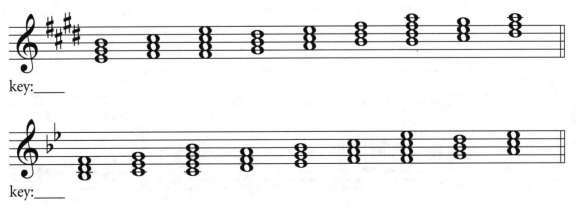

key:____

key:____

Study the following chords built on the D minor scale. These chords are labeled with both functional and root/quality chord symbols.

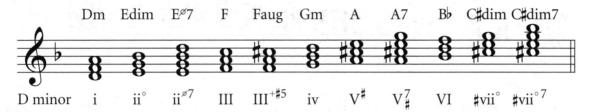

Minor keys are a combination of the natural, harmonic, and melodic minor scales so there are more options for chord choices. This depends on whether the leading note is raised. The chords listed above are some of the more common chords seen in the minor key with the exception of the augmented triad on III. It is included here to illustrate the aug symbol used for an augmented triad, but this chord is fairly rare. The 7th chord built on ii in the minor key is a half-diminished 7th (a diminished triad with a minor 7th), and is symbolized with $^{\varnothing}7$.

Functional chord symbols are used in most traditional academic harmony studies. Understanding root/quality chord symbols is essential to a complete knowledge of chord structure. This text periodically includes root/quality symbols to illustrate and reinforce root and chord quality.

2. For the following chords, name the key, write the functional chord symbols below the staff, and the root/quality chord symbols above the staff.

key:____

key:____

3. The following chords are written in open position, with accidentals instead of a key signature. Write the root/quality chord symbols for each.

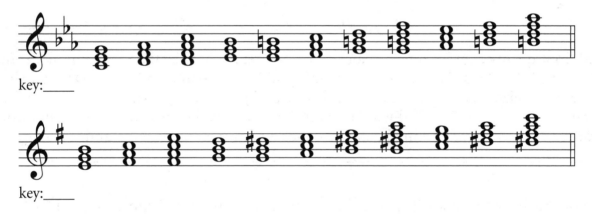

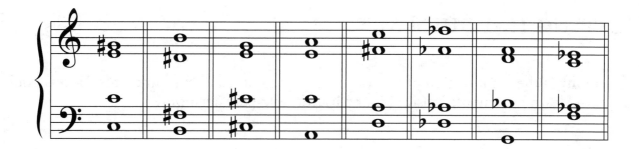

SUMMARY OF LESSON 1

1. Music that is based on a major or minor scale is considered tonal music.

2. The four qualities of triads that are found in major and minor keys are: major, minor, diminished, and augmented.

3. A 7th chord is a four-note chord that is formed by adding the interval of a 3rd to a triad.

4. Functional chord symbols are Roman numerals placed below the staff to identify the root of the chord by the scale degree on which it is built.

5. Uppercase Roman numerals are used for major and augmented chords and lowercase numerals are used for minor and diminished chords. The symbol + indicates an augmented chord and ° indicates a diminished chord.

6. Figured bass symbols specify a chord by its intervallic structure. Alone, they do not name the root of the chord or identify its quality.

7. Root/quality chord symbols identify the root of the chord by its letter name and state the quality of the chord (major, minor, augmented, diminished). They do not indicate the key or the function of the chord within the key.

Lesson 2
Writing in Four Parts

Harmony is the combination of two or more sounds heard at the same time. In this book we will learn to compose music in four parts, or **four-part harmony**.

Four-Part Style

In four-part style—or four-part harmony—chords (triads) are written in four parts. These parts can be the four voices of a choir: **soprano**, **alto**, **tenor**, and **bass**.

The *soprano* part is written for women's or children's high voices.

The *alto* part is written for women's or children's low voices.

The *tenor* part is written for men's high voices.

The *bass* part is written for men's low voices.

These voice names may be abbreviated to **SATB** for convenience.

The following excerpt is written for four-voice choir.

Liebster Jesu, wir sind hier

Johann Sebastian Bach
(1685–1750)

Notice that:

1. The music is written on the grand staff.
2. The soprano and alto are written in the treble staff.
3. The tenor and bass are written in the bass staff.
4. The stems of the soprano and tenor go up, and the stems of the alto and bass go down. This defines each part clearly, so that each singer knows which notes to sing.

In four-part writing, each voice has a specific range that is comfortable for those singers.

When writing in four parts, make sure that each part stays within its range.

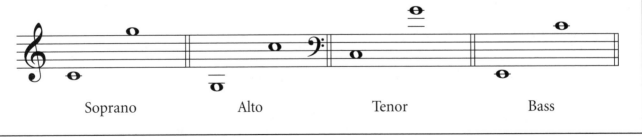

Here are four examples of the tonic chord (I) in G major written for four voices:

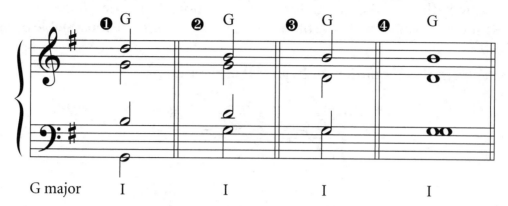

When two voices sing the same note (for example, the tenor and bass in Example ❸ above), two stems are attached to the same notehead. If the two voices sing whole notes (as in Example ❹ above), the two notes are placed side by side.

Chords in Root Position

All chord tones retain their original names—**root**, **third**, and **fifth**—regardless of the position of the chord or the placement of the notes on the staff. In the tonic chord (I) in G major, G is the root, B is the third, and D is the fifth.

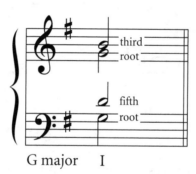

A chord in **root position** always has the **root** in the bass. The other notes may be placed in any order above the root.

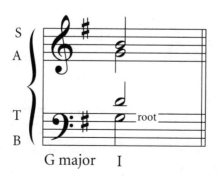

WRITING IN FOUR PARTS

Since four-part writing requires four voices, one of the notes of the triad must be written twice. For now, we will double the root. The root of chord I is the tonic of the key—the strongest and most important note of the key. The root is also the most stable of the three notes of the triad.

Please note, however, that the third must be present in every chord.

G major   I

The space between the soprano and alto, and the alto and tenor, should not exceed one octave. There is no limit to the space between the tenor and bass as long as the notes are within the voice ranges.

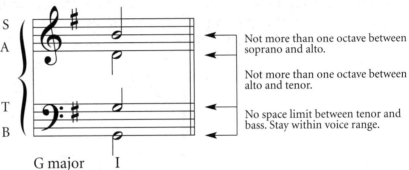

G major   I

Not more than one octave between soprano and alto.

Not more than one octave between alto and tenor.

No space limit between tenor and bass. Stay within voice range.

In four-part writing, each part moves melodically, but the soprano voice is considered the melody. Any note of the triad can function as the melody note.

NOTE: The line after the chord symbol in this example indicates that the chord continues.

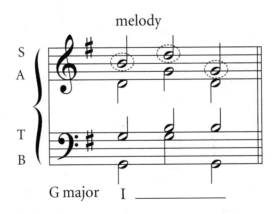

melody

G major   I _____

1. Answer the following questions.

    (a) Name the four voices that make up a mixed choir.

    _____ _____ _____ _____

    (b) Which two voice parts are written on the treble staff?

    _____ _____

    (c) Which two voice parts are written on the bass staff?

    _____ _____

    (d) Which two parts are written with stems going up?

    _____ _____

    (e) Which two parts are written with stems going down?

    _____ _____

    (f) Name the four voice parts and write their ranges.

    _____ _____ _____ _____

    (g) Which notes must be present in every chord?

    _____ _____

    (h) Which voice has the melody in four-part writing?

    _____

    (i) Which chords are symbolized with uppercase or capital Roman numerals?

    _____ _____

    (j) Which chords are symbolized with lowercase or small Roman numerals?

    _____ _____

WRITING IN FOUR PARTS

2. Add the alto and tenor voices to complete the following examples in four-part style. Double the root of each chord.

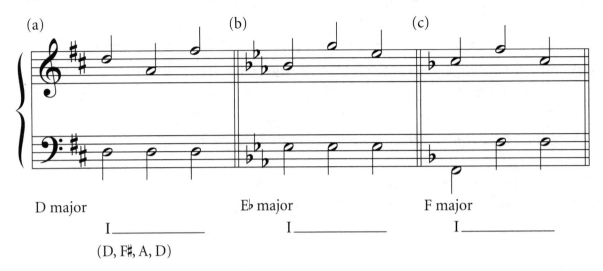

D major

I_____

(D, F♯, A, D)

E♭ major

I_____

F major

I_____

Errors to Avoid in Four-Part Style

Crossed parts occur when two voices exchange position—for example, if the tenor moves above the alto. Although the ranges of adjacent parts overlap, when writing chords in four-part style, it is important to *avoid crossing parts.*

The soprano must be the highest voice. The alto must be the second highest voice, the tenor must be the third highest, and the bass the lowest.

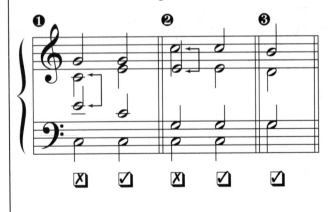

In Example ❶, the tenor E is higher than the C alto. To correct this, put the E in the alto part and the C in the tenor.

In Example ❷, the alto C is higher than the soprano E. Changing the direction of the stems will correct this error.

Example ❸ is correct. Two voices on the same note (here, the tenor and bass) does not constitute crossed parts.

1. Write three different four-part arrangements of the tonic (I) chord in the following keys, above the given bass notes. Write the functional chord symbols under each chord.

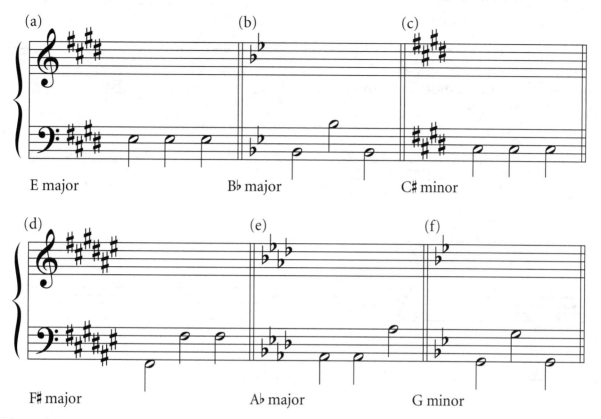

(a) E major   (b) B♭ major   (c) C♯ minor

(d) F♯ major   (e) A♭ major   (f) G minor

Voice-Leading

The term **voice-leading** refers to the melodic movement of a single voice, or two or more voices in combination.

Because SATB harmony is vocal music, much of our writing moves by step or in a scale-like fashion. Smooth voice-leading is important to make the lines singable. Try to avoid large leaps and awkward intervals. Voice lines that move by step are said to be **conjunct**, while voice lines that move in leaps are said to be **disjunct**. A **leap** is a melodic interval of a 3rd or more.

As a general rule, avoid leaps of more than a 4th in the alto and tenor voices.

Voices can move in various ways:

Motion by two voices in the same direction is called **similar motion**.

Motion by two voices in the opposite direction is called **contrary motion**.

Motion by two voices in the same direction and the same numerical interval apart is called **parallel motion**. The qualities of the interval may vary as in the example.

Motion by one voice when the other voice remains stationary is called **oblique motion**.

1. Indicate the type of motion found in the following examples (similar, contrary, parallel, or oblique).

_____   _____   _____   _____

_____   _____   _____   _____

Melodic Motion

In four-part harmony, each voice functions melodically, but the soprano voice, being the highest and most exposed, carries the main **melody**. This melody may repeat a note, move by step, or leap. A combination of these types of motion results in an interesting and effective melody. Stepwise or conjunct motion is common in melodies, but leaps add interest and variety to a line. Too many leaps can create a fractured melody that is hard to sing. The treatment of leaps is an important element in good melodic writing.

The smallest leap is a leap of a 3rd. This is the least disjunct leap and is effective when preceded or followed by stepwise motion or arpeggiation.

A leap of a perfect 4th or 5th is most effective when followed by a change of direction.

Stepwise motion in the same direction after a leap of a perfect 4th or 5th is possible, but not quite as smooth.

A leap of a 6th is most effective if it is followed by motion in the opposite direction. Stepwise motion is best, but a skip is acceptable.

good   good

A leap of a 6th followed by motion in the same direction is poor. A leap of a 6th approached in the same direction is also poor.

poor   poor

good   poor

good

Leaps of more than an octave are not allowed.

A leap of an octave should be approached and left by stepwise motion or triadic skips in the opposite direction. A leap of an octave approached or left by motion in the same direction is poor.

poor   poor

good   good   poor

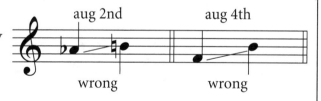

possible

An augmented interval between two melody notes is considered unacceptable.

Two leaps in the same direction are acceptable if the intervals combine to form a chord.

Two leaps adding up to the interval of a 7th are poor and should be avoided.

Two leaps of 4ths are usually poor, but arpeggiation of a dominant 7th can be effective.

aug 2nd   aug 4th

wrong   wrong

2.   Identify and mark the voice-leading errors in the following melodies.

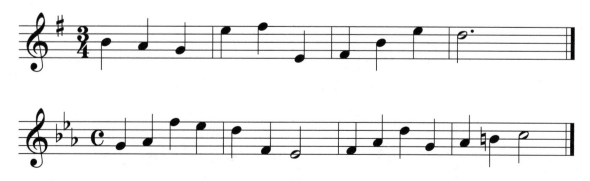

SUMMARY OF LESSON 2

1. The four voices that make up a choir are soprano, alto, tenor, and bass.

2. Soprano and alto are written on the treble staff; bass and tenor are written on the bass staff.

3. In four-part harmony, one note must be doubled in each chord.

4. The root and the third must be present in every chord.

5. The space between the soprano and alto, or between the alto and tenor, must not exceed one octave.

6. Crossed parts occur when two voices exchange position. This must be avoided.

7. As a rule, avoid leaps of more than a 4th in the alto and tenor.

8. Voice-leading refers to the melodic movement of a part alone or in combination with other parts.

9. Two voices in combination can move in four different ways: similar motion, contrary motion, parallel motion, and oblique motion.

10. There are two types of melodic motion: conjunct (stepwise), and disjunct (leaping).

11. A melodic leap of more than an octave is not acceptable.

12. After a large melodic leap, it is best to change direction. Stepwise motion in the opposite direction is effective.

13. Augmented intervals written melodically are considered unacceptable.

LESSON 3
CHORDS I AND V

I–V–I is the most basic **progression** in Western tonal music. The tonic chord (I) is home base for tonal music. Most tonal music begins and ends with the tonic chord.

At the end, just before the tonic chord, there is often a dominant (V) chord. This is known as a **perfect** or **authentic cadence.**

A **cadence** is a place of rest and resolution in music. Cadences are progressions that involve two chords and occur at the end of a phrase or at the end of a piece of music.

The Perfect or Authentic Cadence V–I

The root of each chord is in the bass. The two chords of a perfect cadence have one note in common. This note is called the **common tone.** Here, both chords contain the note C. The easiest way to connect these two chords is to repeat the common tone in the same voice and move the remaining voices stepwise. Notice that the leading note (E) moves to the tonic (F) in the soprano voice. The strongest sounding perfect cadence ends with the tonic (scale degree î) in the soprano. This is called a **closed cadence.**

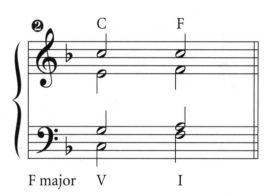

Example ❷ shows the same cadence written differently. The root of each chord is in the bass. The leading note (E) is in the alto and rises to the tonic (F) in the same voice. The common tone (C) is in held the soprano. Since this cadence does not end with the tonic in the soprano, it is called a **semi-closed cadence.**

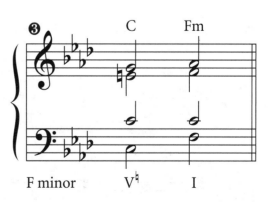

The perfect cadence in a minor key requires an accidental for the raised leading note. The dominant (V) chord in Example ❸ contains an E natural, the raised leading note in F minor. A natural sign beside the V in the figuration is used to indicate a raised third above the bass.

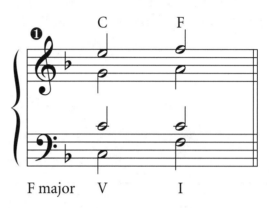

The Imperfect or Half Cadence I–V

An **imperfect** or **half cadence** occurs when a phrase ends on the dominant. This cadence can end a section of a piece, but not the piece itself. The previous rules apply when connecting I to V. The root of each chord is in the bass. The common tone usually stays in the same voice, and the other voices move to the nearest possible notes of the next chord, in this case stepwise. This cadence is an **open cadence.**

Other voice-leading can be used for both the perfect and imperfect cadences, and will be shown later.

1. For the following examples, name the key, symbolize the chords with functional and root/quality chord symbols, and name the cadences as perfect or imperfect.

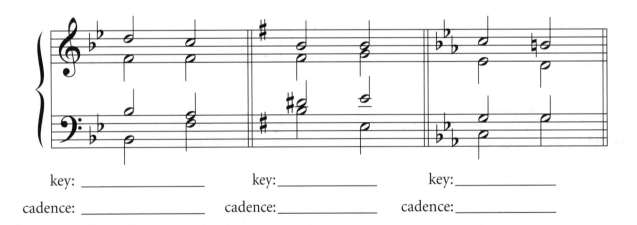

key: _____   key: _____   key: _____

cadence: _____   cadence: _____   cadence: _____

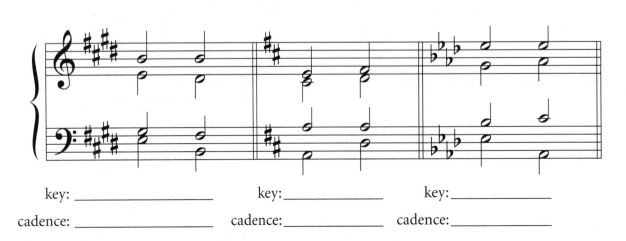

key: _____   key: _____   key: _____

cadence: _____   cadence: _____   cadence: _____

Errors to Avoid in Four-Part Writing

When we write in four parts, certain types of parallel motion between parts are unacceptable. Parallel motion occurs when two voices that are the same numeric interval apart move in the same direction.

Parallel unisons, perfect octaves, or perfect 5ths are not allowed. Compound intervals of these types (perfect 12th and 15th) are also forbidden in parallel motion.

However, if an interval is repeated at the same pitch in two positions of the same chord, or between two different chords, there is no parallel motion. This is acceptable.

Parallel Unisons

Parallel unisons occur when two voices move by unison.

In Example ❶, the parallel unisons occur between the soprano and alto.

In Example ❷, the parallel unisons occur between the alto and tenor.

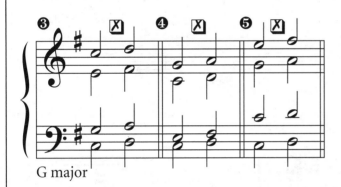

Parallel Perfect Octaves

In Example ❸, parallel octaves occur between the soprano and bass.

In Example ❹, parallel octaves occur between the alto and bass.

In Example ❺, parallel octaves occur between the tenor and bass.

Parallel Perfect 5ths

In Example ❻, parallel 5ths occur between the tenor and bass.

In Example ❼, parallel 5ths occur between the soprano and alto.

In Example ❽, compound parallel 5ths (perfect 12ths) occur between the bass and alto. A perfect 5th followed by a diminished 5th, however, is acceptable.

CHORDS I AND V

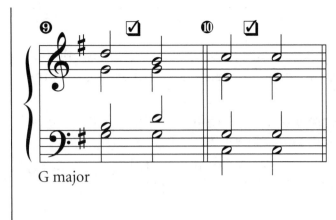

G major

Repeated 5ths and octaves are not wrong. Parallel octaves and 5ths occur only when there is a progression between two different chords. Example ❾ shows repeated octaves between two positions of the same chord. Example ❿ shows repeated 5ths between two positions of the same chord. *Both of these are correct.* However, it is best not to repeat a chord from a weak beat to a strong beat unless the weak beat is an upbeat to a phrase.

1. For each example, name the key, symbolize the chords with functional chord symbols, find and mark any incorrect parallel 5ths, octaves, and unisons, or incorrect crossed parts, spacing problems, and doubled leading notes.

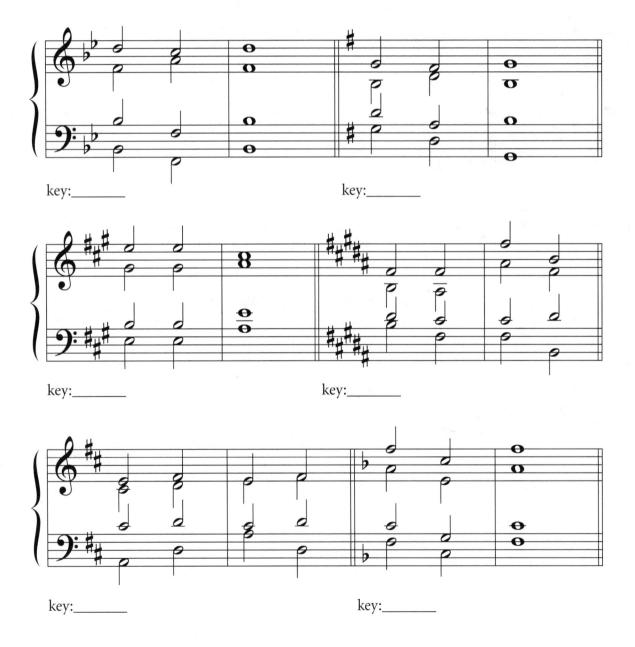

key:_____

key:_____

key:_____

key:_____

key:_____

key:_____

2. Complete the following progressions by adding functional chord symbols and alto and tenor voices.

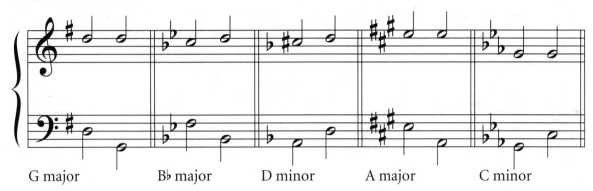

G major   B♭ major   D minor   A major   C minor

3. Write chord progressions in four parts in the following keys. (Each progression ends with a double bar line.)

E minor   V♯   i   i   V♯   A♭ major   V   I   I   V

D major   V   I   I   V   B major   I   V   V   I

D minor   i   V♯   V♯   i   D♭ major   V   I   I   V

Harmonizing a Given Melody Using I and V

Every scale tone can be numbered. The tonic, no matter where it is placed in the octave, is referred to as scale degree $\hat{1}$. A caret sign (^) placed above a number identifies that number as a scale degree.

C major

C melodic minor

You may be given a soprano line and asked to complete the alto, tenor, and bass parts. The most common soprano lines for V and I use scale tones $\hat{1}$ or $\hat{3}$ with chord I, and $\hat{7}$ or $\hat{2}$ with chord V. Scale degree $\hat{5}$ may be harmonized by I or V, depending on the musical context.

The following soprano patterns allow a common-tone connection and/or stepwise motion in the alto and tenor.

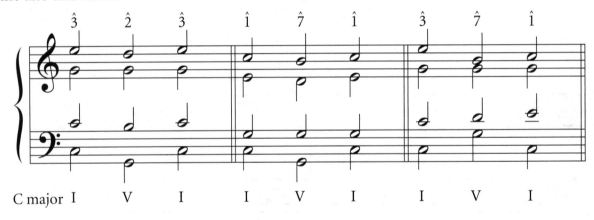

C major   I   V   I   I   V   I   I   V   I

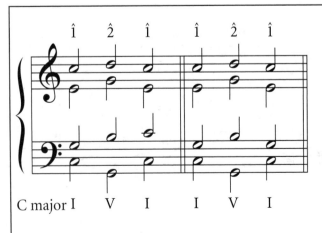

C major I   V   I   I   V   I

In some cases, it is not possible to connect chords I–V–I with a common tone and stepwise motion. Soprano lines using scale degrees $\hat{2}$–$\hat{1}$ with V–I or $\hat{1}$–$\hat{2}$ with I–V do not allow common-tone and stepwise motion. In this case, each part should move to the nearest available note of the next chord and stay within its voice range. Do not allow the alto or tenor to leap more than a 4th in this progression.

1. Number the scale degrees of the following soprano lines. Symbolize the chords with functional chord symbols, then harmonize them in four-part (SATB) style.

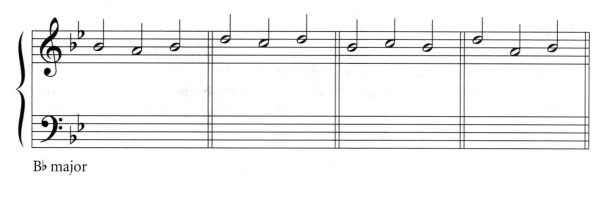

B♭ major

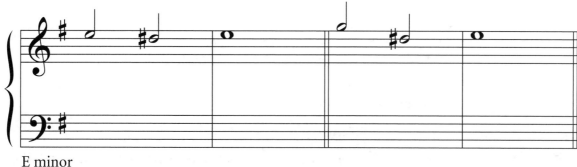

E minor

SUMMARY OF LESSON 3

1. A perfect or authentic cadence consists of the chord progression V–I. This cadence can be closed or semi-closed, depending upon the soprano.

2. The chords I and V share a common tone. The easiest way to connect these chords is to keep the common tone in the same voice and move the other voices stepwise.

3. Parallel motion occurs when two voices that are the same distance apart move in the same direction. Parallel unisons, perfect 5ths, and perfect octaves are not allowed. Compound perfect intervals (perfect 12ths and perfect 15ths) are also not allowed.

4. The easiest way to connect two chords is hold the common tone and use stepwise motion for the other voices. When this is not possible, move each voice to the nearest available note of the next chord. Be sure to follow correct doubling rules and avoid faulty parallels.

5. An imperfect or half cadence occurs when a phrase ends on the dominant. Imperfect cadences are open cadences.

Lesson 4
Pre-dominant Chords IV and ii

We have learned that the most basic harmonic progression is I–V–I. Often this progression is expanded by one or more chords that prepare the dominant chord. The chord that comes before the dominant is called a **pre-dominant chord**. The two root-position chords that most commonly precede the dominant are IV and ii.

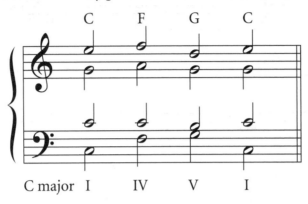

C major   I   IV   V   I

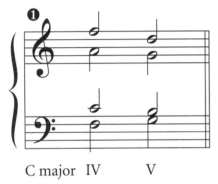

C major IV   V

IV–V

There is no common tone between chords IV and V. *When connecting these two chords, and doubling the root of each, the three upper notes move in contrary (opposite) motion to the bass.*

In Example ❶, the bass rises from F to G. All the other voices in chord IV move in the opposite direction (down) to the nearest available notes of chord V. By moving in this way, faulty parallels are avoided.

In minor keys, the voice-leading shown in Example ❸ must be followed for iv–V, in order to avoid a melodic augmented 2nd. Melodic augmented intervals are unacceptable in any voice part. Example ❷ is incorrect, not only because of the numerous instances of faulty parallel motion between voice parts, but also because of the augmented 2nd from A flat to B natural in the tenor.

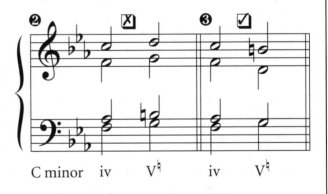

C minor   iv   V♮   iv   V♮

Remember, when two chords in root position have no note in common, the smoothest way to connect them and avoid faulty parallels is to move the soprano, alto, and tenor in contrary motion to the bass. If the bass rises, the three upper voices fall to the nearest available note of the next chord. There are other ways to connect these chords, but this is the smoothest choice, and provides the easiest voice-leading.

1. Name the key of each example and add soprano, alto, and tenor parts to complete the following progressions.

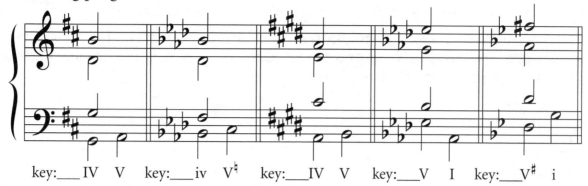

key:___IV V key:___iv V♯ key:___IV V key:___V I key:___V♯ i

2. Name the key of each example and add alto and tenor parts to complete the following progressions.

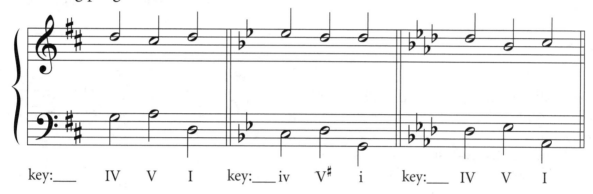

key:___ IV V I key:___iv V♯ i key:___ IV V I

3. Complete the following progressions by connecting the chords in the smoothest correct way.

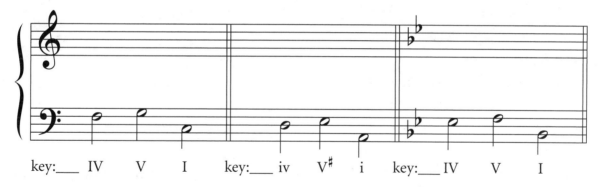

key:___ IV V I key:___ iv V♯ i key:___ IV V I

4. Add soprano, alto, and tenor parts to complete the following progressions.

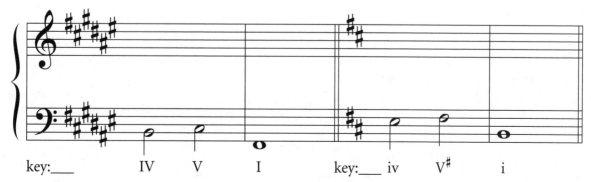

key:___ IV V I key:___ iv V♯ i

Chord ii is an excellent choice for a pre-dominant chord. The best chord to follow ii is V.

In major keys, ii is a minor chord, so it is written with lowercase Roman numerals.

In minor keys, ii is a diminished chord. Because of its harsh sound, it is best to avoid using it in root position. You may double any note (root, third, fifth) in ii, but the root is the most common choice for doubling when ii is in root position.

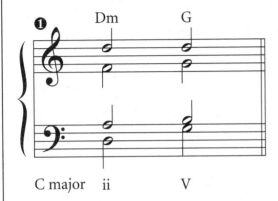

C major   ii   V

ii–V

Chords ii and V share a common tone, so the easiest way to connect them is to keep the common tone in the same voice and move the other voices by step. In Example ❶, the bass moves from the root of ii to the root of V. The soprano keeps the common tone D, and the alto and tenor move stepwise.

C major ii   V   ii   V

Occasionally, a given soprano will not allow common-tone and stepwise motion in the progression ii to V. In this case, the alto and tenor should move to the nearest available chord tones. Be careful to avoid faulty parallels.

Soprano voices using scale degrees $\hat{2}$ and $\hat{7}$, or scale degrees $\hat{4}$ and $\hat{2}$, for the progression ii to V, do not allow for a common-tone and stepwise progression.

Rules to Remember

- If two root-position chords share a common tone, try to keep it in the same voice and move the other voices stepwise.

- If there is no common tone, try to move the upper voices in contrary motion to the bass to the nearest available chord tones.

- If these procedures don't work, follow general voice-leading rules by moving each voice to the nearest available chord tone. Be careful to avoid faulty parallels.

Imperfect Cadences

In this lesson, we have studied the progressions IV–V and ii–V. When a phrase ends on the dominant, there is an imperfect cadence. The progressions studied thus far that form imperfect cadences at the end of a phrase are:

I–V

IV–V

ii–V

1. Complete the following progressions by connecting the chords in the smoothest correct way.

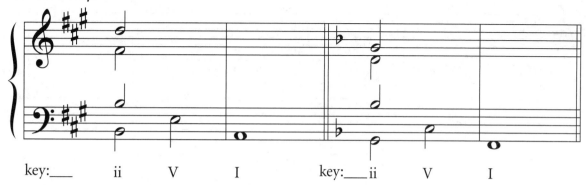

key:___   ii   V   I   key:___ii   V   I

2. The following ii–V progressions do not allow for common-tone stepwise motion. Complete the alto and tenor parts, using correct doubling and avoiding faulty parallels.

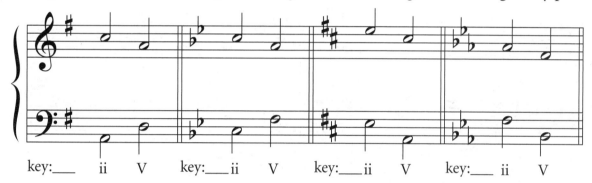

key:___ ii   V   key:___ii   V   key:___ii   V   key:___ ii   V

3. Complete the following progressions by adding soprano, alto, and tenor voices.

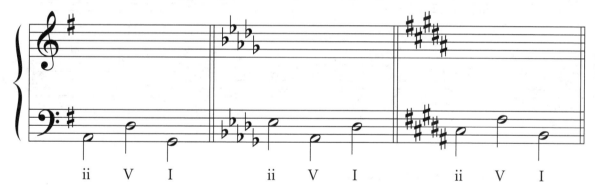

ii   V   I   ii   V   I   ii   V   I

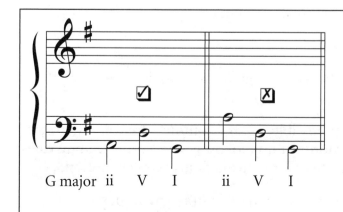

G major ii   V   I   ii   V   I

When writing the progression ii–V–I, it is best to avoid successive leaps in the same direction in the bass.

4. Harmonize the following melodies for four voices.

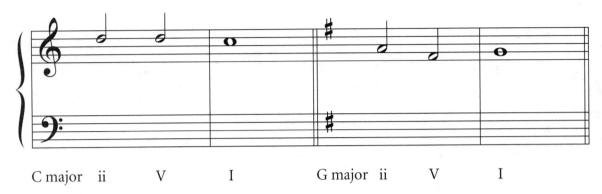

C major   ii   V   I   G major ii   V   I

5. Name the keys and symbolize the following progressions with functional chord symbols.

key:___   key:___

key:___   key:___

SUMMARY OF LESSON 4

1. A pre-dominant chord is a chord that comes before the dominant chord.

2. IV and ii are excellent choices for pre-dominant chords.

3. There is no common tone between IV and V. When writing this progression, move the three upper voices in contrary motion to the bass.

4. The progression ii to V has a common tone. If possible, use the common-tone and stepwise motion in the other voices to connect these chords. If not, follow general voice-leading rules by moving each voice to the nearest available chord tone. Avoid faulty parallel motion.

5. The progressions IV–V, ii–V, and I–V occurring at the end of a phrase are imperfect cadences.

LESSON 5
APPROACHING PRE-DOMINANT CHORDS FROM I

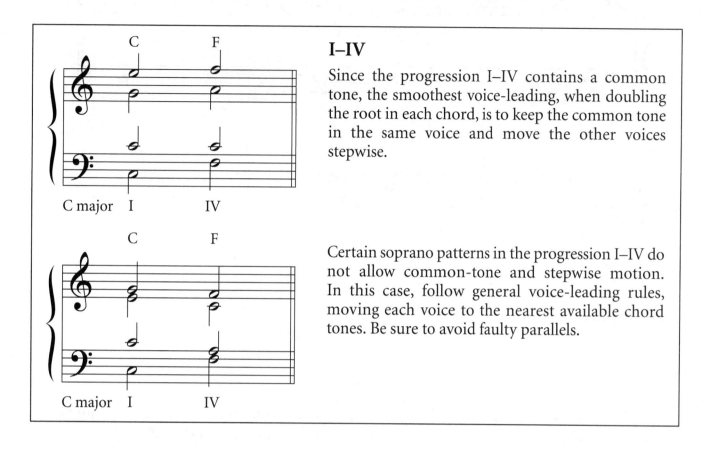

I–IV

Since the progression I–IV contains a common tone, the smoothest voice-leading, when doubling the root in each chord, is to keep the common tone in the same voice and move the other voices stepwise.

Certain soprano patterns in the progression I–IV do not allow common-tone and stepwise motion. In this case, follow general voice-leading rules, moving each voice to the nearest available chord tones. Be sure to avoid faulty parallels.

1. Complete the following progressions in four-part style. Each progression ends with a double bar line.

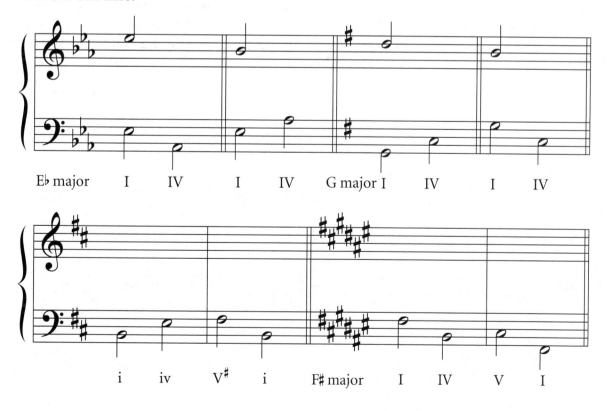

APPROACHING PRE-DOMINANT CHORDS FROM I

Db major   I   IV   V   I   Eb major   I   IV   V   I

Ab major   I   IV   V   I   i   iv   V♯   i

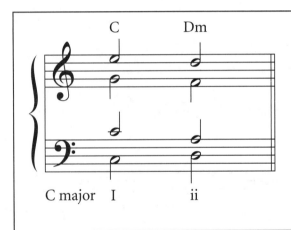

C major   I   ii

I–ii

There is no common tone between chords I and ii. In this progression, the three upper voices move in contrary motion to the bass.

In this example, with doubled roots in both chords, the bass rises, so the soprano, alto, and tenor fall to the nearest available chord tone. When writing this progression, use stepwise motion in the bass rather than a leap of a 7th.

2. Complete the following progressions in four parts for SATB.

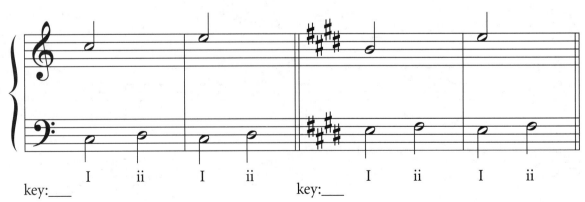

key:___   I   ii   I   ii   key:___   I   ii   I   ii

3. Add soprano, alto, and tenor to complete the following progressions.

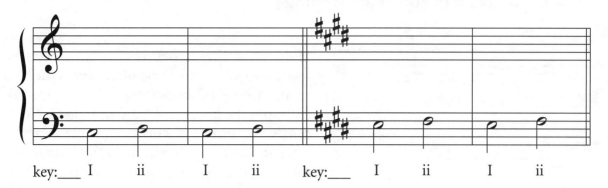

key:___ I ii I ii   key:___ I ii I ii

Harmonizing a Given Melody

The chords we have studied so far support the following scale degrees in the soprano.

I	$\hat{1}, \hat{3}, \hat{5}$
V	$\hat{2}, \hat{7}, \hat{5}$
IV	$\hat{1}, \hat{4}, \hat{6}$
ii	$\hat{2}, \hat{4}, \hat{6}$

---

4. Harmonize the following melodies.

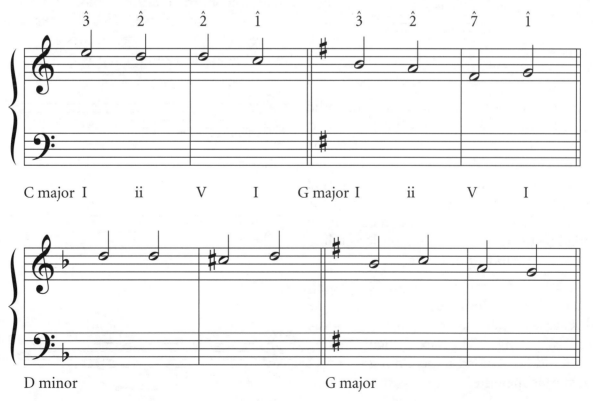

C major I   ii   V   I   G major I   ii   V   I

D minor   G major

More Errors to Avoid in Four-Part Writing

G major

Hidden or **direct octaves** occur when the soprano leaps in the same direction as the bass to an interval of an octave, as in Example ❶. (A leap is the interval of a 3rd or larger.) *This is considered incorrect.* However, if the soprano steps in the same direction as the bass to the interval of an octave, as in Example ❷, it is considered acceptable.

Hidden or **direct 5ths** occur when the soprano leaps in the same direction as the bass to an interval of a 5th, as in Example ❸. *This is considered incorrect.* However, if the soprano steps in the same direction as the bass to the interval of a 5th, as in Example ❹, it is considered acceptable.

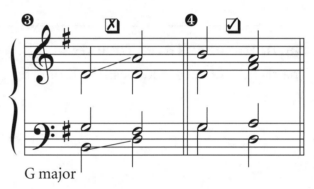

G major

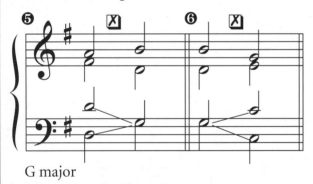

G major

It is not permissible for two voices to move from an octave to a unison, or to move from a unison to an octave. In Example ❺, the tenor and bass move from an octave to a unison. In Example ❻, the tenor and bass move from a unison to an octave. *This is considered incorrect.* The problem here occurs as a result of unnecessary leaps in the tenor.

In four-part vocal music, all melodic augmented intervals, especially the augmented 2nds and 4ths, should be avoided. In major keys, an augmented 4th occurs melodically between $\hat{4}$ and $\hat{7}$. In minor keys with a raised leading note, an augmented 2nd can occur between $\hat{6}$ and $\hat{7}$. Augmented 2nds can be avoided by using the ascending or descending form of the melodic minor scale.

The interval of a melodic major 7th should also be avoided. Composers of the Baroque and Classical periods used these melodic intervals sparingly. They are difficult to sing and should be avoided in beginning exercises or in simple melodic writing.

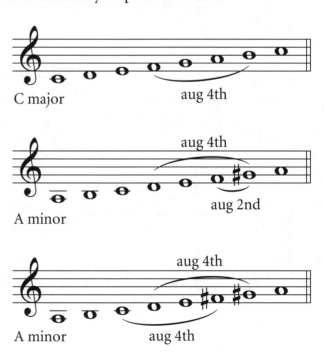

C major — aug 4th

A minor — aug 4th / aug 2nd

A minor — aug 4th / aug 4th

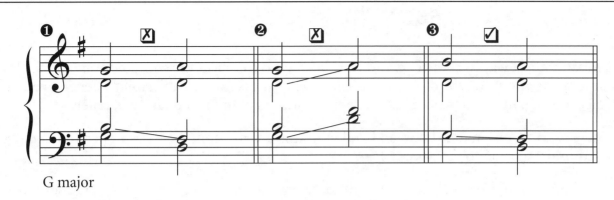

G major

Voices should not cross over one another. This is called **overlapping.**

✔ The soprano note should not move lower than the previous alto note.

✔ The alto should not move lower than the previous tenor note or higher than the previous soprano note.

✔ The tenor should not move lower than the previous bass note or higher than the previous alto note.

✔ The bass should not move higher than the previous tenor note.

In Example ❶, the tenor moves lower than the previous bass note. In Example ❷, the bass moves higher than than the previous tenor note, and the alto moves higher than the previous soprano note. *This is considered incorrect.*

Example ❸ is acceptable because the overlap is approached with stepwise motion. Overlaps, although not completely forbidden, should be avoided in four-part style.

1. Find and mark the voice-leading errors in the following examples. There may be crossed parts, parallel 5ths or octaves, hidden 5ths or octaves, or overlapping parts.

F major

C major

SUMMARY OF LESSON 5

1. The smoothest way to connect chord I to chord IV is to repeat the common tone in the same voice, and move the other voices stepwise. If this is not possible, follow general rules of voice leading; move to the nearest available chord tones and avoid faulty parallels.

2. There is no common tone between I and ii. In this progression, the three upper voices move in contrary motion to the bass.

3. Avoid hidden or direct octaves that occur between the bass and soprano when the soprano leaps in the same direction as the bass to the interval of an octave.

4. Avoid hidden or direct 5ths that occur between the bass and soprano when the soprano leaps in the same direction as the bass to the interval of a 5th.

5. It is not permissible for two voices to move from an octave to a unison, or to move from a unison to an octave.

6. Voice overlap occurs when one voice crosses over another. This should be avoided in four-part writing.

7. Do not write melodic augmented intervals or melodic major 7ths in any voice.

LESSON 6
CHORDS IN FIRST INVERSION

Chords in root position have the root in the bass. A four-note chord with a doubled root in root position contains the intervals of an octave, a 5th, and a 3rd above the bass. In figured bass, compound intervals are expressed as simple intervals (for example, 3 rather than 10 in m. 1 below).

For the tonic chord in C major:

C to C is an octave, C to G is a 5th, and C to E is a 3rd. Roman numerals alone indicate root position.

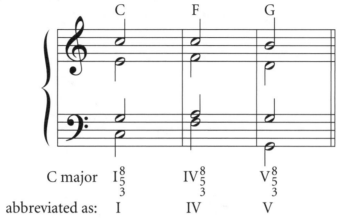

Chords in **first inversion** have the third of the chord in the bass (lowest note). The Arabic numbers used to indicate the intervals above the bass note are 6 and 3. For the tonic chord in first inversion in C major: E to C is a 6th, and E to G is a 3rd. When symbolizing first-inversion chords, omit the number 3 and write the symbols as:

$$I^6 \quad IV^6 \quad V^6$$

Other names for first-inversion chords are **six-three chord** or **chord of the sixth**. Study the root/quality chord symbols for these chords. They are written with the root and quality of the chord followed by a slash and the note that is in the bass. For example, the first inversion of C major is written as C/E. This indicates a C major chord with E as the lowest note.

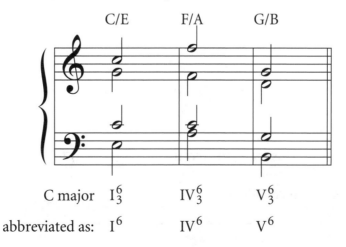

Any note of a first-inversion chord may be doubled except the leading note found in V^6.

ii⁶ as a Pre-Dominant Chord

The chord ii⁶ is an effective pre-dominant. This chord is closely related to chord IV because it has two notes in common (scale degrees $\hat{4}$ and $\hat{6}$) and shares the same bass note. In minor keys, ii°⁶ is effective, but root-position ii° is harsh and should be avoided.

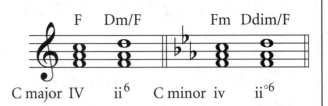

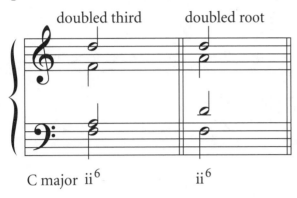

The chords ii and ii⁶ contain scale degrees $\hat{2}$, $\hat{4}$, and $\hat{6}$. These two chords can harmonize soprano scale degrees $\hat{2}$ and $\hat{4}$, but rarely a soprano scale degree $\hat{6}$.

Although you can double any note in ii⁶, and it is common to double the root, it is usually best to double the third, which is found in the bass.

1. Complete the following ii⁶ chords.

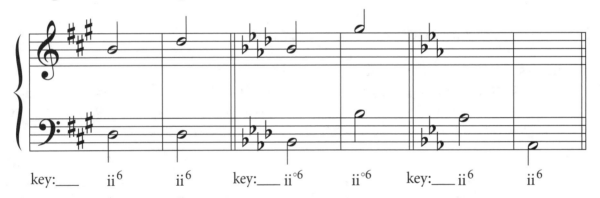

ii⁶–V

Although there is a common tone between ii⁶ and V, common-tone and stepwise movement is not recommended.

In this progression, the three upper voices should move in contrary motion to the bass to the nearest available chord tones.

It is important to follow this rule to avoid faulty parallel motion. This progression at the end of a phrase is an imperfect cadence.

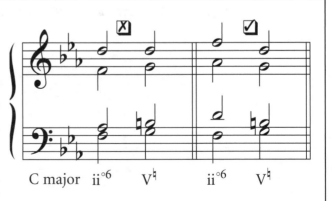

For the progression ii°⁶–V in minor keys, voice-leading rules must be followed carefully to avoid a melodic augmented 2nd.

The upper voices should move in contrary motion to the bass to the nearest available chord tones.

Example ❶ is incorrect, not only because of the parallel octaves between the bass and alto, but also because there is a melodic augmented 2nd in the soprano from A flat to B natural.

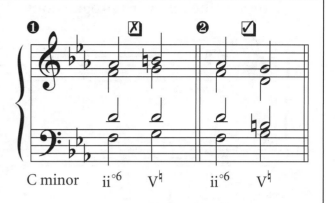

2. Complete the following progressions according to the chord symbols.

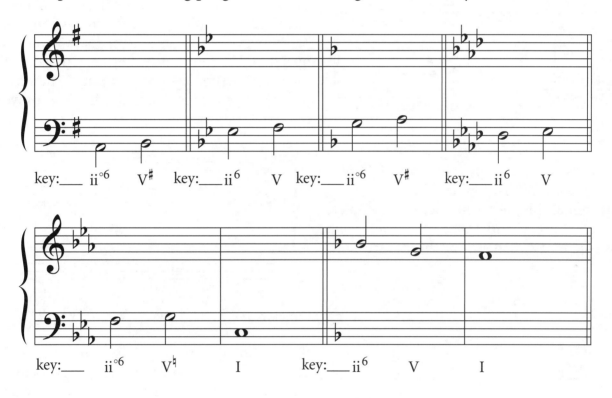

I–ii⁶

There is no common tone between I and ii⁶. To write this progression, follow general voice-leading rules by moving to the nearest available chord tone, using correct doubling and avoiding faulty parallels.

3. Complete the following progressions.

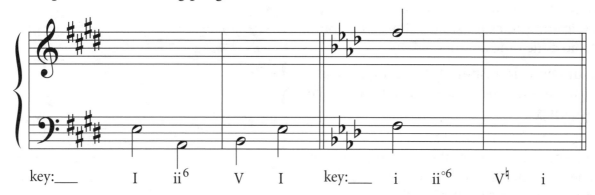

key:___   I   ii⁶   V   I   key:___   i   ii°⁶   V♮   i

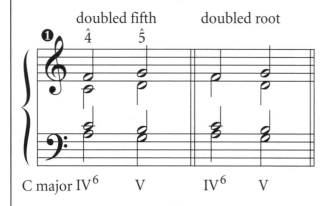

doubled fifth   doubled root

$\hat{4}$ $\hat{5}$

C major IV⁶   V   IV⁶   V

Stepwise motion is possible from IV⁶–V if the fifth of IV⁶ is doubled. In Example ❷, the remaining notes needed to complete chord V are B and D. Be careful to avoid crossed parts when writing this progression.

C major IV⁶   V   IV⁶   V   IV⁶   V

IV⁶ as a Pre-dominant Chord

The chord IV⁶ can function as a pre-dominant. The soprano that most occurs with IV⁶–V uses scale degrees $\hat{4}$ and $\hat{5}$. In this progression, the bass moves down a step and the soprano moves up a step. The root of IV⁶ may be doubled, but the smoothest voice-leading occurs when the fifth of the chord is doubled. All voices move by step.

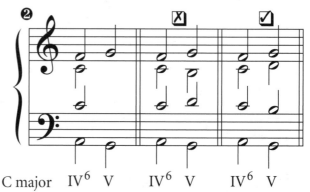

C major   IV⁶   V   IV⁶   V   IV⁶   V

Be careful also to avoid incorrect spacing between the alto and tenor. In Example ❸, the remaining notes of chord V (B and D) must be placed carefully to avoid faulty spacing.

If a phrase ends with the progression IV⁶–V, it is considered an imperfect cadence. In minor keys, the cadence iv⁶–V is a **Phrygian cadence**.

iv⁶–V in Minor Keys

In minor keys, a melodic augmented 2nd can be avoided by doubling the root or the fifth of iv⁶.

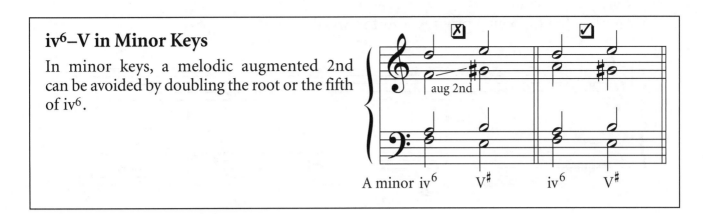

4. Complete the following IV⁶–V progressions.

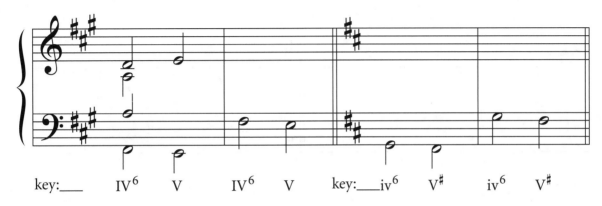

I–IV⁶

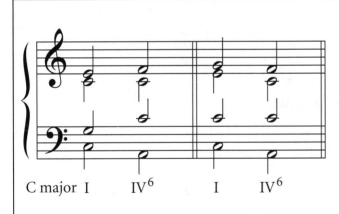

The best movement for this progression is to repeat the common tone between I and IV⁶ in the same voice. Here, IV⁶ has scale degree 4̂ in the soprano. The fifth of IV⁶ is doubled. One of the inner voices may have to leap the interval of a 4th, depending upon the soprano note used in chord I.

5. Write the following I–IV⁶ progressions in four parts for SATB. Use scale degree 4̂ in the soprano for chord IV⁶.

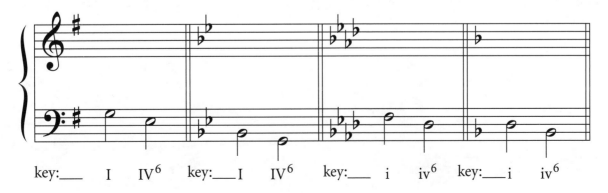

6. Complete the following progressions for SATB.

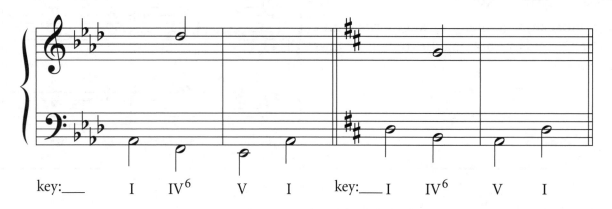

key:___ I IV⁶ V I   key:___ I IV⁶ V I

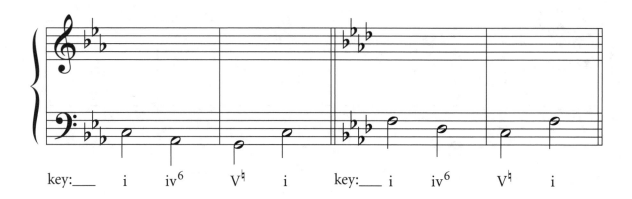

key:___ i iv⁶ V♮ i   key:___ i iv⁶ V♮ i

SUMMARY OF LESSON 6

1. Chords in first inversion have the third in the bass and are symbolized with the figure "6" (I⁶, IV⁶, V⁶, etc.).

2. The chord ii⁶ is a common pre-dominant in both major and minor keys.

3. The smoothest voice-leading between ii⁶ and V occurs when the upper notes move in contrary motion to the bass.

4. IV⁶ can function as a pre-dominant. In the progression IV⁶ to V, the root of IV⁶ may be doubled, but the smoothest voice-leading occurs when the fifth of IV⁶ is doubled.

5. The progression IV⁶–V is an imperfect cadence. In minor keys, the cadence iv⁶–V is a Phrygian cadence.

Lesson 7
The Dominant 7th Chord

The **dominant 7th chord**—V^7—can take the place of V in the basic harmonic progression I–V–I: I–V^7–I. The dominant 7th, like V, is built on the fifth degree of the scale, but has an added 7th above the root. The intervals that make up a dominant 7th chord are a major 3rd, a perfect 5th, and a minor 7th. V^7 has two dissonant elements: the 7th, and the diminished 5th or augmented 4th that occurs between the third and seventh.

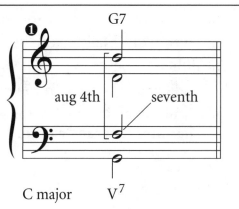

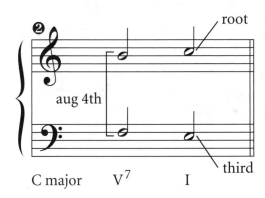

When V^7 resolves to I, the notes of the augmented 4th should move stepwise to the chord tones of I. The seventh of V^7 (F) falls to the third of chord I (E). The seventh is an active tone and is known as a **tendency tone**. A tendency tone is an unstable tone that tends to move toward a stable tone. Tendency tones pull to the nearest note of the tonic triad. For example, the leading note pulls or resolves to the tonic. Tendency tones should not be doubled. If you double the leading note, you will have two voices pulling in the same direction, and parallel octaves will occur if both voices move to the tonic.

When the notes in Example ❶ are inverted, the interval of a diminished 5th occurs (as in Example ❸). The notes of this diminished 5th resolve inward by step to chord tones of I. The interval of an augmented 4th or diminished 5th is formed between scale degrees $\hat{4}$ and $\hat{7}$. These two scale degrees are the strongest tendency tones of the major key because they are only one semitone away from the root and third of the tonic triad (I).

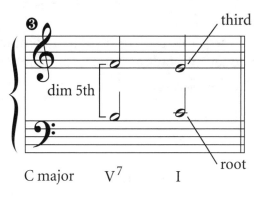

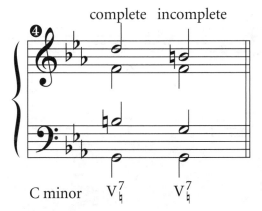

V^7 may be written as a complete chord containing the root, third, fifth, and seventh, or as an incomplete chord by doubling the root and omitting the fifth.

THE DOMINANT 7TH CHORD

The progression V⁷–I is a perfect cadence. There are three ways to resolve V⁷.

Method 1:

The root of V⁷ moves to the root of I.

The seventh of V⁷ falls a step.

The fifth of V⁷ falls a step.

The leading note (scale degree $\hat{7}$) rises to the tonic.

This results in an incomplete tonic (I) chord that contains three roots and a third.

Method 2:

The root of V⁷ moves to the root of I.

The seventh of V⁷ falls a step.

The fifth of V⁷ falls a step.

The leading note (scale degree $\hat{7}$) moves down a third to the dominant (scale degree $\hat{5}$).

This results in a complete tonic (I) chord with a doubled root.

In this example, the diminished 5th does not resolve normally. This voice-leading produces a stronger sonority because of the complete I chord. *Note that when the leading note ($\hat{7}$) is in the soprano, it must rise to the tonic ($\hat{1}$).*

Method 3:

An incomplete V⁷ resolves to a complete chord I. The seventh falls and the leading note rises.

The doubled root of V⁷ is kept as a common tone.

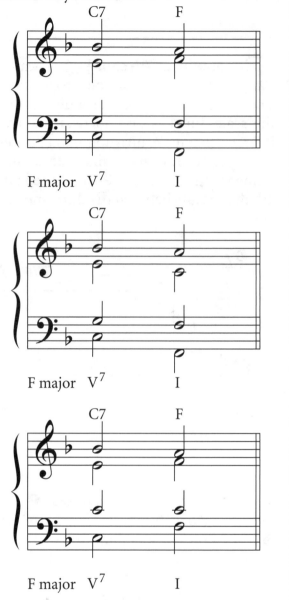

1. Resolve the following V⁷ chords.

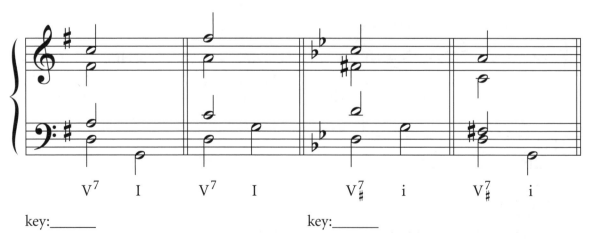

key:_____   key:_____

The pre-dominant chords IV, ii, and ii⁶ are excellent chords to precede V⁷. The seventh of the dominant 7th is scale degree $\hat{4}$. All three pre-dominant chords contain this note. The seventh of V⁷ is often approached as a common tone from IV, ii, or ii⁶. When the seventh of V⁷ is approached as a common tone, it is said to be **prepared**.

IV–V⁷

The smoothest way to connect IV and V⁷ is to prepare the seventh as a common tone and move the other voices, in contrary motion to the bass, to the nearest available chord tones. This results in an incomplete V⁷ that has a doubled root, a third, and a seventh. Motion other than this can result in faulty parallels or, in minor keys, a melodic augmented 2nd.

1. Complete the following progressions in four-part style.

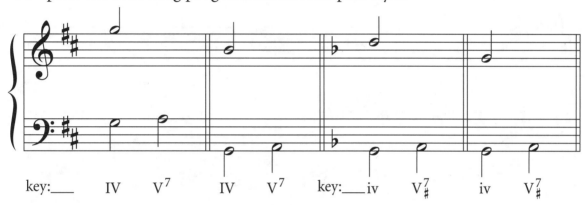

ii and ii⁶–V⁷

The best way to connect ii and ii⁶ to V⁷ is to prepare the seventh as a common tone and follow the normal voice-leading rules by moving to the nearest available chord tones and avoiding faulty parallels. The V⁷ chord may be complete or incomplete depending on which scale degrees are in the soprano. Because the supertonic chord in a minor key is diminished, do not use it in root position. Example ❸ shows the use of ii° in first inversion: ii°⁶. This also shows the usual voice-leading with ♭$\hat{6}$ falling in one voice and raised $\hat{7}$ approached from above in another voice. Example ❹ shows the less common version of this progression using raised $\hat{6}$. This changes the quality of the supertonic triad to minor (ii⁶). The minor ii triad may be used in root position in minor keys.

Study the following examples. Depending upon the soprano, some progressions allow two common tones to be repeated.

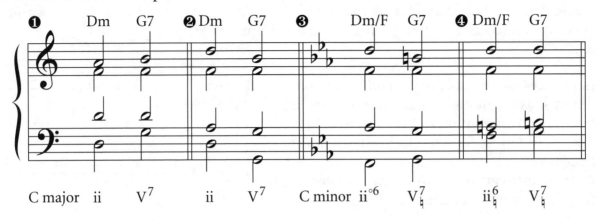

1. Complete the following progressions.

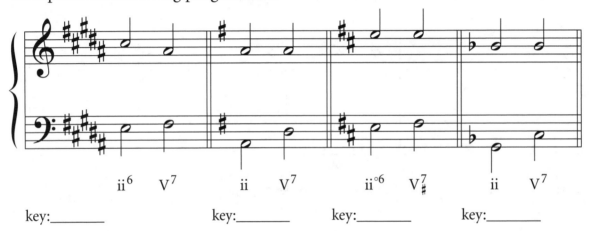

key:_____   key:_____   key:_____   key:_____

Approaching V^7

Preparing the seventh of V^7 as a common tone is a good approach, but this is not always possible. The seventh of V^7 may also be approached by step or from below by leap. Remember that a perfect 5th followed by a diminished 5th is not faulty parallel motion.

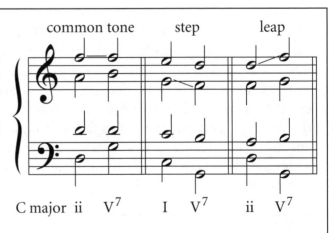

2. Complete the following progressions for SATB.

SUMMARY OF LESSON 7

1. The dominant 7th is built on the fifth degree of the scale, and can take the place of V in the basic harmonic progression of I–V–I.

2. One way to prepare the seventh of V^7 is to hold it as a common tone from the pre-dominant chord.

3. The seventh of V^7 (scale degree $\hat{4}$) is a strong tendency tone, and usually resolves downward to scale degree $\hat{3}$ in chord I.

4. The leading note in V^7 may resolve by rising to the tonic. This progression creates an incomplete I chord with three roots and a third. The leading note may also fall by a 3rd to the dominant (scale degree $\hat{5}$) if it is in an inner voice. This creates a complete I chord with a doubled root.

5. V^7 may be written as a complete chord (root, third, fifth, and seventh) or as an incomplete chord (doubled root, third, and seventh).

6. An incomplete V^7 always resolves to a complete I chord.

Lesson 8
Harmonic Analysis 1

Harmonic analysis involves naming keys and identifying and symbolizing chords with functional chord symbols, root/quality chord symbols, or both.

Non-Chord Tones

When analyzing a passage of music, we often find notes that are not part of the underlying harmony or chord structure. These notes are called **non-chord tones**, **non-harmonic tones**, or **decorative notes**. They are used to decorate the melody, and provide rhythmic interest and motion. These notes are classified by the way in which they are approached and left, and by their metrical position.

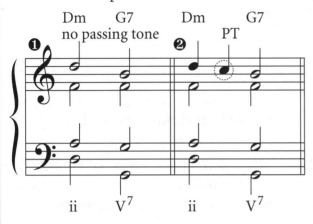

Passing tones can occur in more than one voice at the same time if they move in parallel 3rds or 6ths, or in contrary motion.

Passing Tones

A **passing tone** (**PT**) or **passing note** is a non-chord tone that joins two chord tones that are a third apart. Passing tones are approached and left by step in the same direction. In Example ❷, C is a passing tone between two chord tones D and B. Passing tones can occur in any of the four voices (SATB).

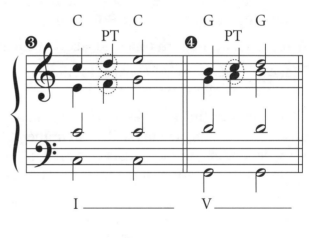

Two passing tones can fill in the interval of a fourth (as in Example ❺). A **chromatic passing tone** (**Chr. PT**) fills in the space of a whole tone.

The passing tone in Example ❻ moves by chromatic semitone (E–E flat).

All the passing tones in these examples are **unaccented**. This means that they fall on a weaker beat or on a weaker part of the beat than the note to which they move (the note of resolution).

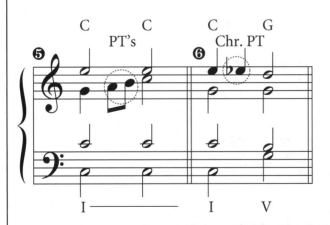

An **accented passing tone** (**APT**) is a passing tone that falls on a stronger beat or on a stronger part of the beat than the note of resolution. An accented passing tone is always approached and left by step. It always moves by step to the chord tone it has displaced.

When adding passing tones, care must be taken to avoid faulty parallels. In Example ❾, the added passing tone creates parallel 5ths between the soprano and alto.

Analyzing a Four-Part Score

Harmonic analysis involves studying a piece of music, and understanding the chords and how they work together.

The first step is to identify the key of the piece. Think about each chord and what chord it is in the key of the piece (an F major chord, a D minor chord, a C major chord, etc.). Then assign the appropriate Roman numeral and, if necessary, the figured bass symbol.

Circle each non-chord tone and label it with an abbreviation of the non-chord name.

Make a legend on the page to indicate what the initials of abbreviation stands for (for example, PT = passing tone).

In minor keys, the raised leading note, and occasionally the raised submediant, is indicated by an accidental sign next to the Roman numeral. This may be a sharp, a double sharp, or a natural sign, depending on the actual accidental in the key. If the accidental appears by itself, it always indicates an alteration of the third of the chord.

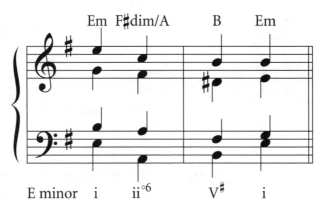

In this example, the tonic chord is symbolized with a lowercase Roman numeral (i) because it is a minor chord. A sharp sign placed next to the V chord indicates the raised leading note. The leading note (D♯) is the third of chord V. *When an accidental sign is placed next to a Roman numeral with no other number, it always refers to the third.* Root/quality chord symbols are placed above the staff.

1. Analyze the following examples: name the keys, symbolize the bass, and circle and identify any passing tones. Use both functional and root/quality chord symbols.

key:_____   key:_____

key:_____   key:_____

Neighbor Tones

A **neighbor tone** (NT) is a non-chord tone that moves one step above or below a chord tone and then returns to the chord tone. Another name for a neighbor tone is **auxiliary note**. Neighbor tones generally occur on weak beats or on weak parts of beats, and may be a whole tone or a semitone away from the chord tone. If a neighbor tone occurs on a stronger beat or part of a beat than the following chord tone, it is called an **accented neighbor tone** (ANT). When two or more neighbor tones occur at once, they should move in parallel 3rds or 6ths or in contrary motion.

A **lower neighbor** moves below the chord tone (Example ❶).

An **upper neighbor** moves above the chord tone (Example ❷).

In Example ❸, two neighbors move in 6ths.

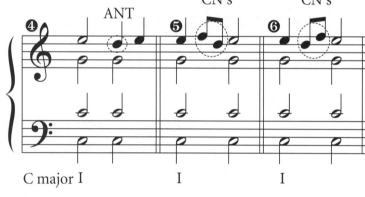

In Example ❹, an accented neighbor tone falls on the beat or strong part of the beat.

Double neighbors—also known as **changing notes** (CN's)—move by step from the chord tone, skip in the opposite direction, and then step back to the chord tone (see Examples ❺ and ❻).

2. Analyze the following examples: name the keys, add functional chord symbols, and circle and identify any non-chord tones.

key:_____   key:_____

Analyzing a Piano Score

The nature, ranges, and capabilities of instruments differ from those of voices, and the writing differs as well.

Piano scores vary greatly in accompaniment patterns and figurations. In four-part music, chords often change on every beat. In piano music, a chord may last for a complete measure or several measures. In a piano score, notes may be missing from chords. When you analyze piano music, you need to look at the key and decide what harmony is implied or suggested by the composer.

A piece may begin with a single note pickup in the first measure. It is important to assign a chord symbol to this note to indicate the implied harmony. Many pickup measures begin with tonic harmony (I), but sometimes V may be implied. It may be useful to see if the opening note is repeated later on and check if it is harmonized in a fuller texture.

The following example illustrates a few typical left-hand piano lines. Beneath each bass line is a harmonic reduction that shows the basic chord structure.

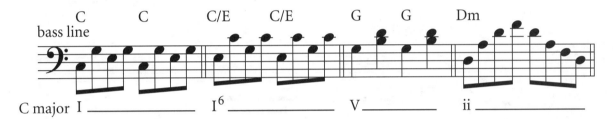

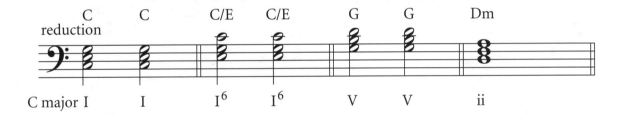

This example is the opening of the *Sonatina in C major,* op. 36, no. 1 by Muzio Clementi. Here, the composer implies tonic harmony. Clementi decided to use a single C in the left hand (perhaps because he wanted a simpler sound than a full chord would provide). The broken-chord melody in the right hand, using the notes of a C major triad, clarifies the implied tonic harmony (I).

Study the following analysis of a piano sonatina by Carl Czerny.

Sonatina

Carl Czerny
(1791–1857)

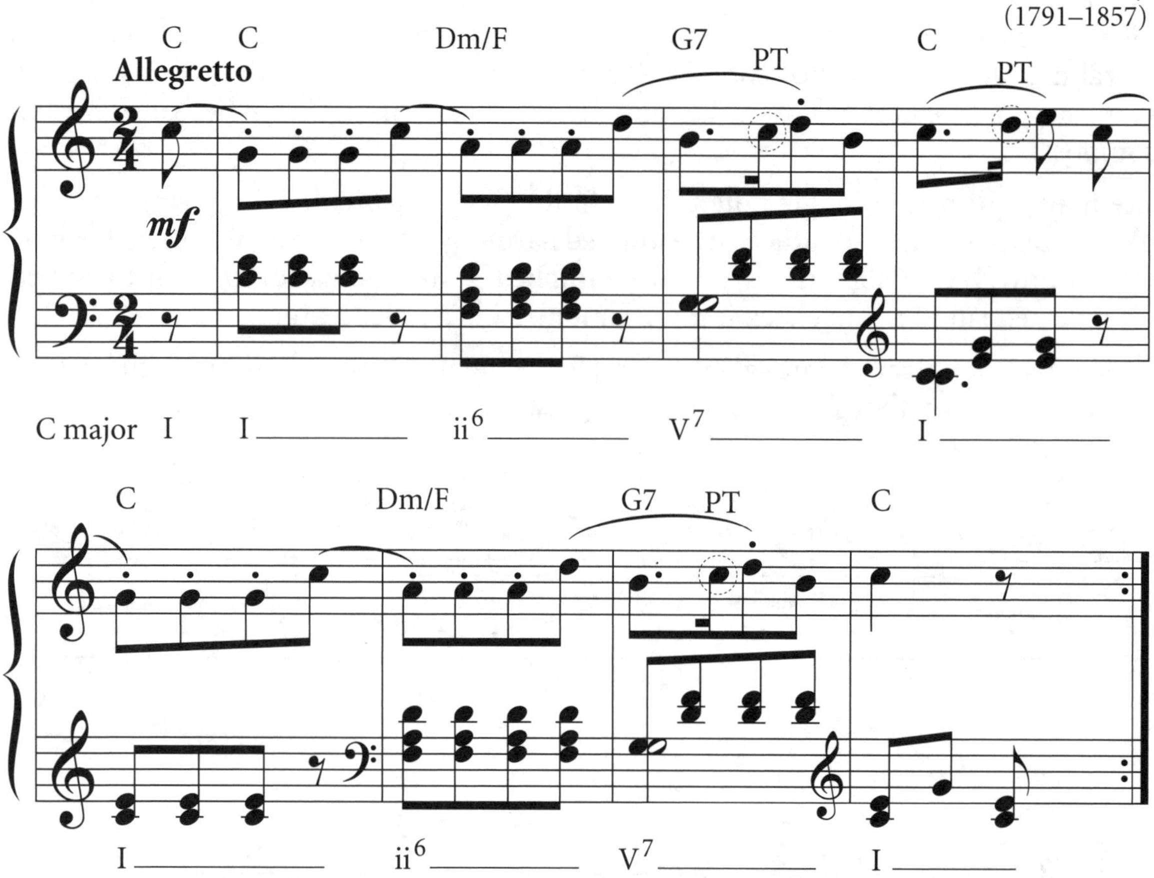

PT = passing tone

In this sonatina, you can determine the chords by looking at the entire measure in both treble and bass clefs. The first note in the bass clef determines the chord position. In m. 3, the notes G B D F indicate V^7. The first note of the measure in the bass indicates the position. Here, G as the first note indicates root position. In m. 4, C E G is the root position of I in C major. The upbeat C in the incomplete measure at the beginning implies chord I. Most upbeats imply either I or V. Any notes that are not part of the harmony, such as C in m. 3, and D in the right hand in m. 4, must be circled and identified as passing tones, neighbor tones, etc. A legend is included at the bottom to show that PT is the abbreviation for passing tone.

3. Provide a harmonic analysis of the following examples. Name the keys, symbolize the chords with functional chord symbols, and circle and identify any non-chord tones.

Vivace
op. 117, no. 8

Cornelius Gurlitt
(1820–1901)

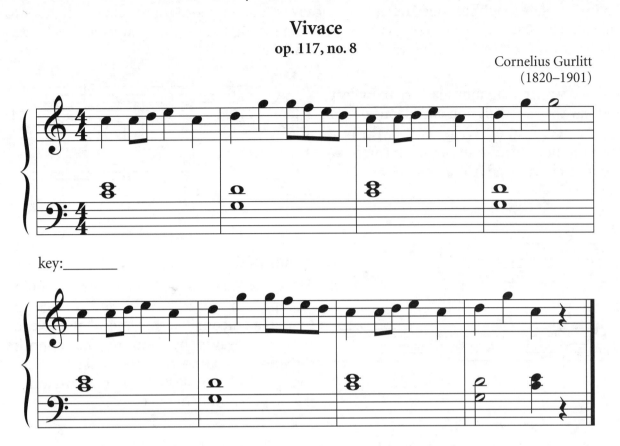

key:_____

from Sehnsucht nach dem Frühling
K 596

Wolfgang Amadeus Mozart
(1756–1791)

key:_____

Incomplete Neighbors

An **incomplete neighbor tone** (**IN**) is a metrically weak non-chord tone that is a neighbor to only one chord tone. Neighbors move by step, but an incomplete neighbor either arrives by step and leaves by leap, or arrives by leap and leaves by step.

An incomplete neighbor may arrive by leap and leave by step. This non-chord tone occurs on a weaker beat or weaker part of the beat than the note of resolution. In Example ❶, the non-chord tone A is a neighbor only to the B.

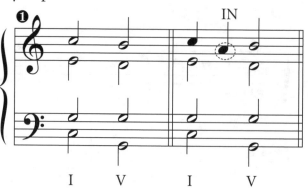

I   V   I   V

I   V   I   V

Échappée

Échappée (**Ech**) is a French word meaning "escape." In music, an *échappée* (or escape tone) is an incomplete neighbor that arrives by step and leaves by leap in the opposite direction. It almost always occurs in the soprano. In Example ❷, the non-chord tone D is a neighbor only to the C.

4. Provide a harmonic analysis of the following. Name the keys, symbolize the chords using both functional and root/quality chord symbols, and circle and identify any non-chord tones.

Sonatina in C major
no. 5 of 12 Sonatines progressives

(a)

Johann Baptist Vaňhal
(1739–1813)

key:_____

Sonatina
(3rd movement)

(b)

Matthew Camidge
(1758–1844)

key:_____

SUMMARY OF LESSON 8

1. Non-chord tones are notes that are not part of the underlying harmony or chord structure. They are used to decorate a melody and provide rhythmic interest and motion.

2. A passing tone joins two chord tones that are a 3rd apart. Two passing tones may fill in the interval of a 4th. A chromatic passing tone moves by chromatic semitone and fills in the space of a whole tone. Passing tones are approached and left by step in the same direction.

3. An accented passing tone is a passing tone that falls on the beat or strong part of the beat. Accented passing tones are approached and left by step in the same direction.

4. An unaccented neighbor tone moves a step above or below a chord tone and then returns to the chord tone. A neighbor tone occurring on a strong beat or strong part of the beat is called an accented neighbor tone.

5. Double neighbor tones, or changing notes, move by step from the chord tone, skip in the opposite direction, and then step back to the chord tone.

6. An incomplete neighbor is an unaccented non-chord tone that is a neighbor to only one chord tone. It either arrives by step and leaves by leap, or arrives by leap and leaves by step.

7. An *échappée* is an unaccented non-chord tone that arrives by step and leaves by leap in the opposite direction.

REVIEW OF LESSONS 1–8

1. The smoothest way to connect two chords that share a common tone (I–V, ii–V, or I–IV) is to double the root in each chord, keep the common tone in the same voice, and move the other voices stepwise.

2. The smoothest way to connect two chords that do not share a common tone (IV–V or I–ii) is to double the root in each chord and move the three upper voices to the nearest available chord tones in contrary motion to the bass.

3. Certain progressions with a common tone (for example, ii⁶–V) do not follow common-tone stepwise motion. To allow for a doubled third and avoid faulty parallels, move to the nearest available chord tones in contrary motion to the bass. Faulty parallel motion can be avoided if the root is doubled and the common tone is repeated in the same voice.

4. Sometimes, because of a particular soprano line, the common-tone stepwise voice-leading may not apply. In such cases, follow the general rules of voice-leading by moving to the nearest available chord tones, avoiding faulty parallels.

5. When connecting a pre-dominant chord to V^7, it is best to prepare the seventh of V^7 by repeating it as a common tone and moving the other notes to the nearest available chord tones.

6. When resolving a complete V^7, the seventh falls and the leading note rises, creating an incomplete I chord with three roots and a third. Another option to this resolution is to have the leading note fall a 3rd, creating a complete I chord with a doubled root. This option is only possible when the leading note is in an inner voice. An incomplete V^7 resolves to a complete chord I. The doubled root of V^7 is repeated as a common tone in chord I.

7. Here is a list of chords and the soprano scale degrees they support.

I	$\hat{1}, \hat{3}, \hat{5}$
V	$\hat{2}, \hat{5}, \hat{7}$
V^7	$\hat{2}, \hat{4}, \hat{5}, \hat{7}$
IV	$\hat{1}, \hat{4}, \hat{6}$
ii	$\hat{2}, \hat{4}, \hat{6}$
ii⁶	$\hat{2}, \hat{4}, \hat{6}$

1. Complete the following progressions in four parts according to the given symbols, bass lines, or soprano melodies.

LESSON 9
PROLONGING CHORD I

The opening tonic chord in the basic harmonic progression (I–V–I) can be expanded or prolonged. A chord that is expanded is called a **prolongation** or an **expansion**.

One way of prolonging chord I is to repeat it. You can change the soprano note to add interest and variety to the prolongation.

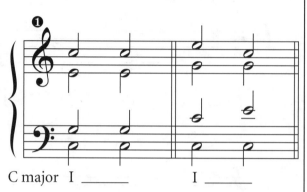

C major I _____ I _____

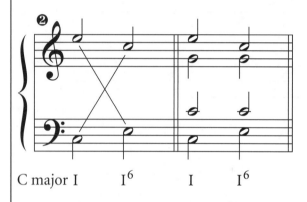

C major I   I^6 I   I^6

Voice Exchange

Another way to prolong chord I is to follow it with I^6. An effective way to do this is to use a technique called **voice exchange**. In Example ❷, the soprano and bass exchange notes. The bass sings C–E and the soprano sings E–C.

For the smoothest voice-leading in this progression, keep the alto and tenor as common tones and double the root in I^6.

Parallel Motion in 10ths

You can prolong chord I with I^6 by moving the soprano and bass in parallel 10ths. If you double the fifth in I^6, the alto and tenor can hold common tones. Although there are other options, this is the smoothest voice-leading for this progression.

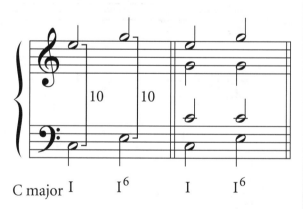

C major I   I^6 I   I^6

1. Complete the following progressions prolonging I.

IV, ii, or ii⁶ can be used as pre-dominant chords to follow a tonic prolongation I–I⁶. Follow general voice-leading rules for these progressions: move to the nearest available chord tones and avoid faulty parallels. These examples illustrate the smoothest possible voice-leading. (Other options are available but those shown allow for the closest movement between voices.)

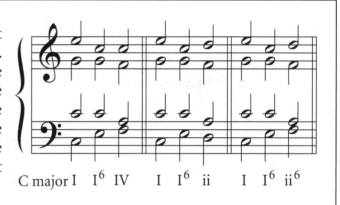

2. Complete the following progressions by adding alto and tenor.

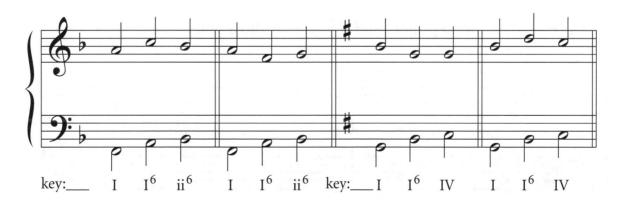

Prolonging Chord I

3. Complete the following progressions by adding soprano, alto, and tenor.

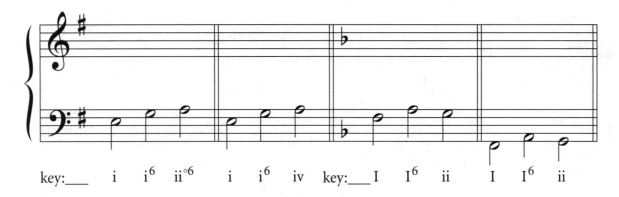

key:___   i   i⁶   ii°⁶   i   i⁶   iv   key:___ I   I⁶   ii   I   I⁶   ii

Chord V may follow the tonic prolongation I–I⁶. At the end of a phrase, this progression will be an imperfect cadence.

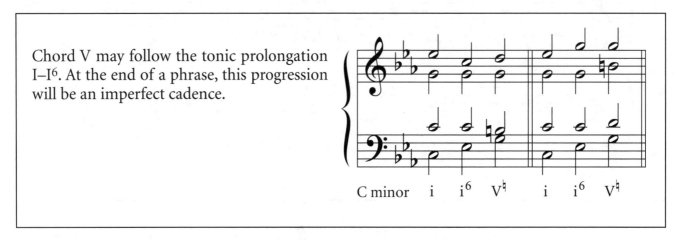

C minor   i   i⁶   V♮   i   i⁶   V♮

4. Complete the following progressions by adding soprano, alto, and tenor.

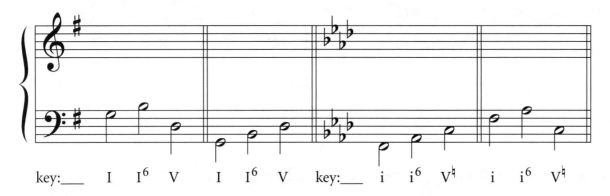

key:___   I   I⁶   V   I   I⁶   V   key:___ i   i⁶   V♮   i   i⁶   V♮

5. Complete the following progressions by adding alto and tenor.

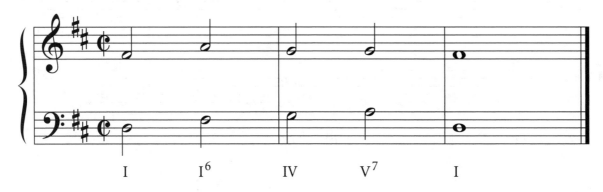

I   I⁶   IV   V⁷   I

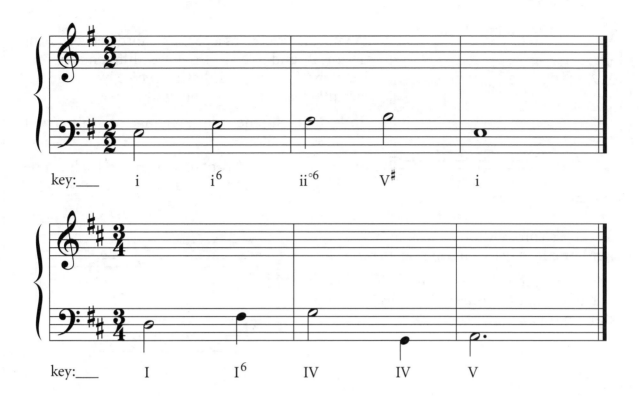

key:___   i   i⁶   ii°⁶   V♯   i

key:___   I   I⁶   IV   IV   V

Prolonging I with vii°⁶

Because the leading-note chord vii° is a diminished chord, it is normally used only in first inversion rather than root position. The vii°⁶ chord is best used as a prolongation of tonic harmony between I and I⁶ or I⁶ and I. Notice the bass in Example ❶. The vii°⁶ acts as a **passing chord** between I and I⁶. The voice exchange between I and I⁶ is filled in with passing tones CDE–EDC.

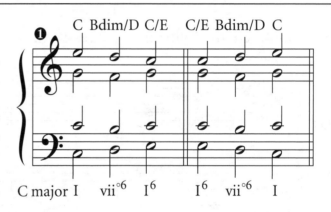

In vii°⁶, it is best to double the third of the chord, that is, the bass note. Do not double the leading note in this progression.

Note that 5ths between the tenor and alto in these examples are not faulty parallels because one is a diminished 5th (B–F) and the other is a perfect 5th (C–G).

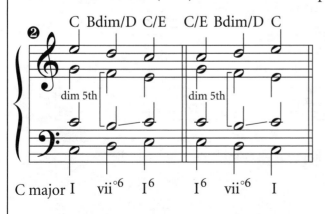

The chord vii°⁶ contains two active scale degrees, $\hat{4}$ and $\hat{7}$, which form the interval of a diminished 5th (tritone). These tendency tones may resolve in the same way that they do in V⁷—$\hat{7}$ moves to $\hat{1}$, and $\hat{4}$ moves to $\hat{3}$. This resolution results in a I or I⁶ chord with two roots and two thirds.

PROLONGING CHORD I

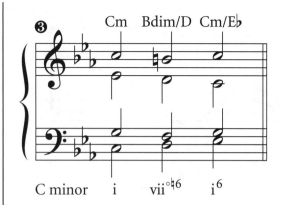

Cm   Bdim/D   Cm/E♭

C minor   i   vii°♮6   i⁶

A vii°⁶ that is used as a passing chord between I and I⁶, or I⁶ and I, can also have different soprano patterns. This means that the voice exchange will occur between the bass and another voice.

In Example ❸, the voice exchange occurs between the bass and alto.

In minor keys, vii°⁶ contains the raised leading note which is shown in the figuration.

A vii°⁶ can also prolong tonic harmony by acting as a **neighbor chord** between two statements of I.

In Example ❹, the bass functions as a neighbor tone. Notice that the other voices also move in neighbor motion.

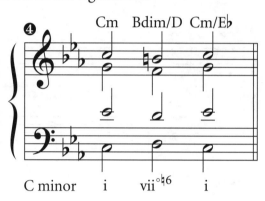

Cm   Bdim/D   Cm/E♭

C minor   i   vii°♮6   i

6. Complete the following progressions.

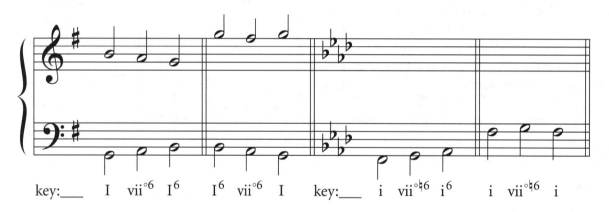

key:___   I   vii°⁶   I⁶   I⁶   vii°⁶   I   key:___   i   vii°♮6   i⁶   i   vii°♮6   i

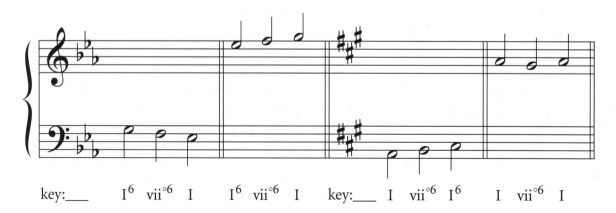

key:___   I⁶   vii°⁶   I   I⁶   vii°⁶   I   key:___   I   vii°⁶   I⁶   I   vii°⁶   I

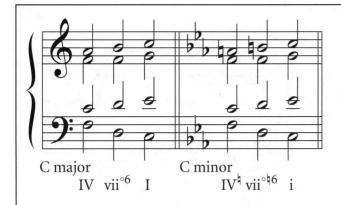

C major
IV vii°6 I

C minor
IV♮ vii°♮6 i

A vii°6 can have a dominant function because it contains three of the tones found in V^7. (For example, in C major, vii° = BDF and V^7 = GBDF.) The progression vii°6–I in both major and minor keys can function as a perfect cadence. This cadence will be semi-closed. Because it has a weaker effect than a V–I perfect cadence, it may be found at the ends of phrases, but not as a final cadence at the end of a piece.

This C minor example uses the melodic form of the minor scale, thus avoiding the melodic augmented 2nd that would otherwise occur in the soprano voice.

7. Complete the following progressions.

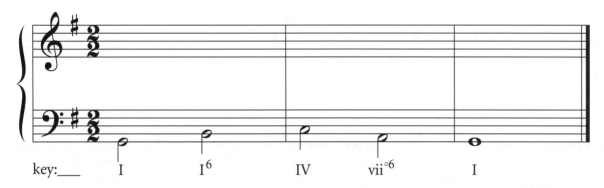

key:___   I I^6 IV   vii°6   I

Prolonging I with V6

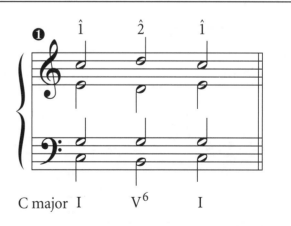

V^6 can be used as a neighbor chord between two positions of I to prolong tonic harmony. In Example ❶, the bass moves in neighbor motion. The tenor holds a common tone, and the soprano and alto move by step in neighbor motion. Here, the smoothest voice-leading comes by doubling the fifth in V^6. However, it would also be acceptable to double the root and have a leap in one of the inner voices.

❶   1̂   2̂   1̂

C major I V^6 I

In minor keys, V⁶ in this progression has the raised leading note in the bass. When the leading note is an outer voice, it resolves upward by step to the tonic. Notice that the accidental occurring in the bass (V⁶) is not figured.

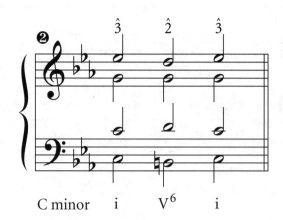

C minor   i   V⁶   i

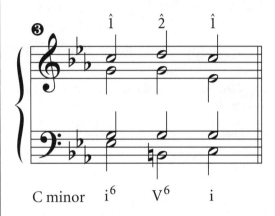

C minor   i⁶   V⁶   i

V⁶ can also be used between I⁶ and I to prolong tonic harmony. In Example ❸, the bass moves by a leap of a 4th and then a step. This makes V⁶ an **incomplete neighbor chord**. In this progression, either the root or the fifth of V⁶ may be doubled. The leading note in the bass resolves upward by step to the tonic.

Be careful when you write the bass line for the progression I⁶–V⁶–I. After a leap, it is better if the bass moves by step in the *opposite direction*.

C major I⁶   V⁶   I   I⁶   V⁶   I
                                        weak

In these progressions, V⁶ has a different role than a V or V⁷ that occurs before the closing tonic. Here, V⁶ is used to prolong or expand the opening tonic. V and V⁷ before the closing tonic have a cadential function. The progression V⁶–I can also have a cadential function. At the end of a phrase, it will serve as a perfect cadence, but this progression is not strong enough to close a piece. The last two chords of a composition should be in root position.

8.   Complete the following progressions.

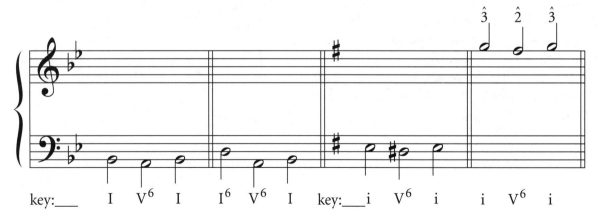

key:___   I   V⁶   I   I⁶   V⁶   I   key:___i   V⁶   i   i   V⁶   i

9. Analyze the following progressions by naming the keys and providing functional chord symbols. Circle and identify any non-chord tones.

key:_____

key:_____

key:_____

key:_____

PROLONGING CHORD I

1. Determine the key of the melody.

   If the given melody has more than one phrase, determine where each phrase ends. Phrases are often four measures long.

2. Choose the cadences for the end of each phrase.

   The final cadence of a melody is usually a perfect cadence (V–I), but imperfect cadences are often used at the end of phrases. It may be helpful to number the scale degrees of the melody. Often the chords you choose for the melody will be influenced by the cadence. Because of this, it is important to choose the cadence first.

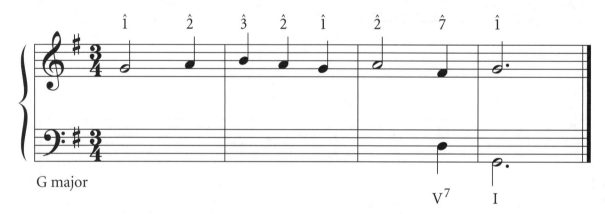

3. Choose a pre-cadential chord.

   It is best if this chord is different from the two cadence chords. Good choices for pre-cadential chords are ii, ii⁶, IV, or IV⁶. An inversion such as I⁶ may also be used.

4. Choose the first chord. An opening chord is often I, or perhaps V.

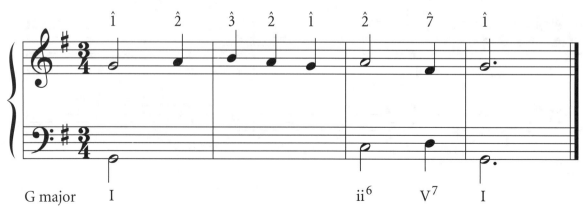

5. Fill in the remaining bass notes.

    Look for patterns in the melody that can support chord progressions that you have learned (for example, I–V⁶ or I–vii°⁶–I⁶). Moving the bass in contrary motion to the soprano is effective and will help to avoid parallel 5ths and octaves. If the leading note appears in the soprano, harmonize it with V or vii°⁶. The voice-leading of the bass line is important. It should have a melodic contour and should not be too disjunct, even though it may well have more leaps than the upper voices. Inverted chords (I⁶, IV⁶, etc.) help to smooth out the bass line and add tonal variety. Check for parallel 5ths and octaves between the bass and soprano before adding the alto and tenor.

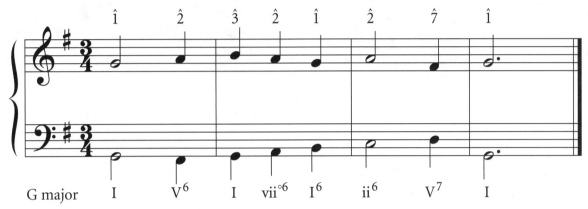

6. Add the alto and tenor to complete the harmonization.

    Be careful to avoid parallel 5ths and octaves.

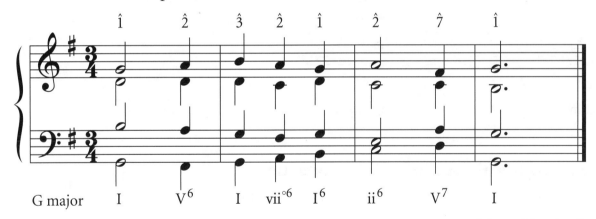

Johann Sebastian Bach
Ach wie nichtig, ach wie fluchtig

Tips

1. If a melody leaps from a strong beat to a weak beat, try harmonizing both notes with the same chord.

2. If a melody note repeats, change the chord or position of the chord, unless repeated chords are a unifying motive in the piece or they occur at the cadence.

3.   Do not repeat a chord after a bar line except:

(a) at the start of a piece

G major I   I   V⁶ I   IV⁶

(b) after a long note

G major I⁶ V   I   I   IV⁶ V   IV⁶

(c) after a rest

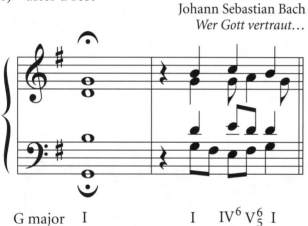

G major   I   I   IV⁶ V⁶₅ I

Harmonizing a Melody in Tonic Prolongation

Here are some soprano patterns that support tonic prolongation.

1̂ 2̂ 3̂	3̂ 2̂ 1̂	1̂ 7̂ 1̂	1̂ 2̂ 1̂	3̂ 2̂ 3̂
I⁶–vii°⁶–I	I–vii°⁶–I⁶	I–vii°⁶–I⁶	I–V⁶–I	I–V⁶–I
I–V⁶–I	I–V⁶–I	I⁶–vii°⁶–I	I⁶–V⁶–I	
I⁶–V⁶–I		I–vii°⁶–I		

10. Provide functional chord symbols and harmonize the following melodic fragments using tonic prolongation.

B♭ major

D minor

Harmonizing $\hat{5}$–$\hat{6}$–$\hat{7}$–$\hat{1}$

An ascending melody consisting of $\hat{5}$–$\hat{6}$–$\hat{7}$–$\hat{1}$ can be harmonized with I–IV–V–I, but this requires downward leaps in the inner voices to avoid faulty parallels. Sometimes leaps in inner voices are both necessary and correct. In Example ❶, a passing tone in the alto between F and D will create a smoother line.

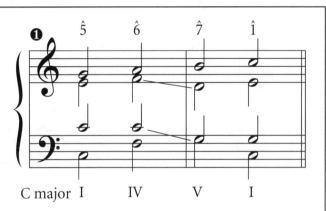

C major   I   IV   V   I

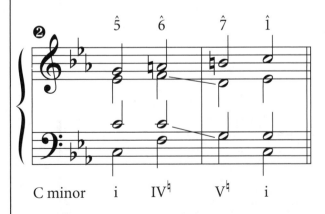

C minor   i   IV♯   V♯   i

$\hat{5}$–$\hat{6}$–$\hat{7}$–$\hat{1}$ in Minor Keys

In minor keys, it is necessary to use the melodic form of the minor scale in order to avoid a melodic augmented 2nd in the soprano.

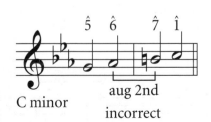

C minor

aug 2nd
incorrect

PROLONGING CHORD I

The melodic progression $\hat{5}$–$\hat{6}$–$\hat{7}$–$\hat{1}$ may also be harmonized using the progression I–IV–vii⁶–I. Here, vii⁶ acts as a substitute for V, creating a perfect cadence. In minor keys, this progression requires a raised $\hat{6}$ to avoid a melodic augmented 2nd.

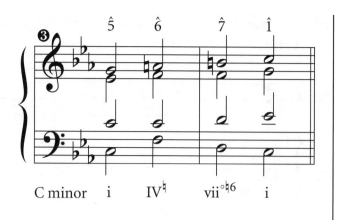

11. Complete the following for four parts by adding alto, tenor, and bass.

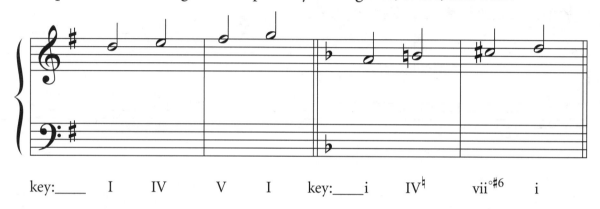

key:____ I   IV   V   I   key:____i   IV♮   vii°♯6   i

12. Complete the following soprano lines in four parts for SATB. Add functional chord symbols.

B♭ major

C minor

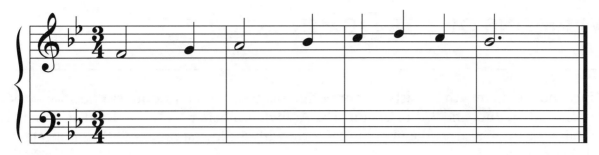

Bb major

SUMMARY OF LESSON 9

1. The opening tonic of the progression I–pre-dominant–V–I is often prolonged with I⁶.

2. A vii°⁶ can be inserted between repetitions of I, or between I and I⁶, to prolong tonic harmony.

3. V⁶ can be inserted between repetitions of I, or between I⁶ and I, to prolong tonic harmony.

4. The melodic progression $\hat{5}$–$\hat{6}$–$\hat{7}$–$\hat{1}$ can be harmonized with I–IV–V–I. In this progression, the inner voices leap downward.

5. $\hat{5}$–$\hat{6}$–$\hat{7}$–$\hat{1}$ may also be harmonized with I–IV–vii⁶–I.

Lesson 10
Inversions of the Dominant 7th

Since the dominant 7th consists of four notes, this chord has four different positions: root position, 1st, 2nd, and 3rd inversion. The Arabic numbers next to the Roman numerals symbolize the intervals that the upper notes form with the lowest note, and thus indicate the position of the chord.

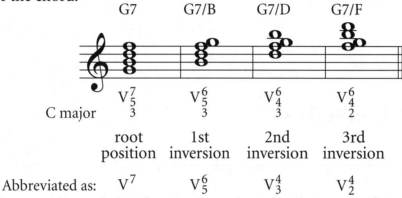

Here is the figuration for the dominant 7th chord in minor keys.

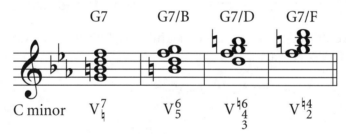

A dominant 7th in root position always has the root in the bass. In first inversion, the 3rd is in the bass, in second inversion, the 5th is in the bass, and in third inversion, the 7th is in the bass. The notes in the upper parts of V^7 may appear in any order above the bass. Inversions of V^7 are always complete chords containing the root, third, fifth, and seventh.

1. Write the following inversions of V^7 for SATB.

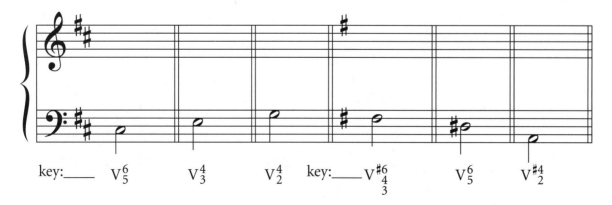

Prolonging I with Inversions of V^7

Inversions of V^7 can be used to prolong an opening tonic.

V^7 and its inversions contain two strongly active tones. These tendency tones must resolve in a particular way. The leading note has a tendency to rise to the tonic, and usually does so if it occurs in the bass or soprano in this progression. The seventh of V^7 has a tendency to fall to the third of chord I.

Prolonging I with V^6_5

V^6_5 is a first-inversion chord and has the leading note in the bass. When the leading note is in the bass, it rises to the tonic (I). Thus, V^6_5 is always followed by I. V^6_5 often occurs as a neighbor chord to I.

Here are four progressions using V^6_5 in tonic prolongation. Notice how the soprano lines differ, and how the leading note rises and the seventh falls.

V^6_5 can also be used to prolong tonic harmony between I^6 and I. In this example, V^6_5 functions as an **incomplete neighbor chord**. Notice that the fifth is doubled in I^6. The leading note rises and the seventh falls. After the bass leaps a 4th, it steps in the opposite direction.

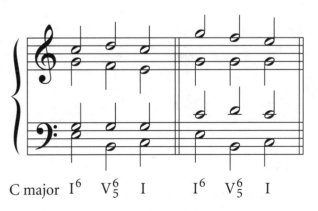

2. Complete the following progressions in four parts for SATB.

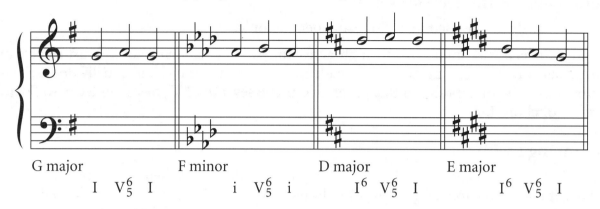

G major	F minor	D major	E major
I V$_5^6$ I	i V$_5^6$ i	I^6 V$_5^6$ I	I^6 V$_5^6$ I

Prolonging I with V$_3^4$

So far, in all progressions involving V^7 and its inversions, the seventh has resolved downward by step. In the progression V$_3^4$–I^6, the bass takes the note to which the seventh would normally resolve (the third of I). When this happens, the seventh may rise to the nearest chord tone. This is considered an **exceptional resolution**.

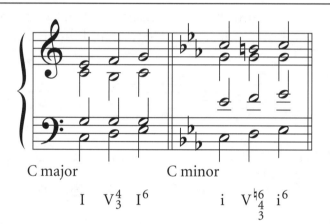

C major	C minor
I V$_3^4$ I^6	i V$_{4\,3}^{\flat6}$ i^6

V$_3^4$ can also be used to prolong tonic harmony in the progression I^6–V$_3^4$–I. Here, the soprano and bass move in parallel 10ths, and the seventh resolves normally.

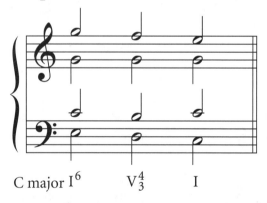

C major I^6 V$_3^4$ I

In the progression I–V$_3^4$–I, V$_3^4$ acts as a neighbor chord between two statements of I. Here, the voices resolve normally, with the seventh falling and the leading note rising.

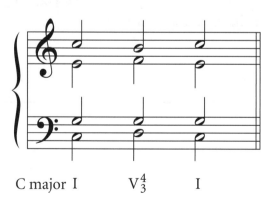

C major I   V$_3^4$ I

3.   Complete the following progressions for SATB.

key:____ I V$^4_3$ I^6 I V$^4_3$ I   key:____I^6 V$^4_3$ I   I V$^4_3$ I^6

key:____ i V$^{\flat 6}_{43}$ i   i V$^{\flat 6}_{43}$ i^6 key:____i V$^{\sharp 6}_{43}$ i^6 i V$^{\sharp 6}_{43}$ i

---

Prolonging I with V$^4_2$

Since V$^4_2$ has the seventh in the bass, and the seventh resolves downward by step, this chord always moves to I^6. V$^4_2$ in tonic prolongation occurs between I and I^6 as an incomplete neighbor chord or as a neighbor chord between two I^6 chords. Notice that in the progression I–V$^4_2$–I^6, the bass steps in the opposite direction after the leap of a 4th.

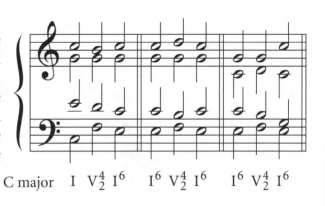

C major   I V$^4_2$ I^6 I^6 V$^4_2$ I^6 I^6 V$^4_2$ I^6

4.   Complete the following progressions for SATB.

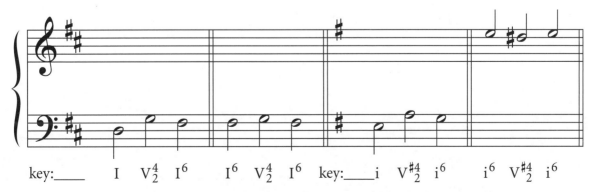

key:____ I V$^4_2$ I^6 I^6 V$^4_2$ I^6 key:____i V$^{\sharp 4}_2$ i^6 i^6 V$^{\sharp 4}_2$ i^6

You have studied the following progressions that prolong the tonic chord (I).

$I-I^6$	$I-vii^{\circ 6}-I^6$	$I-V^6-I$	$I-V^6_5-I$	$I-V^4_3-I^6$	$I-V^4_2-I^6$
I^6-I	$I^6-vii^{\circ 6}-I$	I^6-V^6-I	$I^6-V^6_5-I$	$I^6-V^4_3-I$	$I^6-V^4_2-I^6$
	$I-vii^{\circ 6}-I$			$I-V^4_3-I$	

Here are some helpful rules for writing these progressions:

1. Double the third (bass note) of $vii^{\circ 6}$. Never double the leading note.

2. Double either the root or fifth of V^6.

3. All inversions of V^7 must be complete chords containing the root, third, fifth, and seventh.

4. V^6_5 always moves to I.

5. V^4_2 always moves to I^6.

6. When resolving inversions of V^7, the leading note rises and the seventh falls—with the one exception of $I-V^4_3-I^6$ where one voice (usually the soprano) moves using scale degrees $\hat{3}$ $\hat{4}$ $\hat{5}$.

The progressions listed above may be connected to form longer tonic prolongations.

For example, $I-vii^{\circ 6}-I^6$ can be connected to $I^6-V^6_5-I$ to form a more extensive tonic prolongation: $I-vii^{\circ 6}-I^6-V^6_5-I$.

5. Complete the following progression by adding soprano, alto, and tenor.

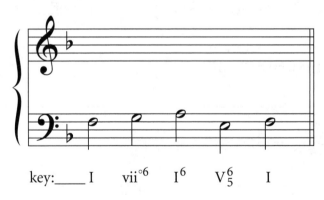

key:____ I   vii$^{\circ 6}$ I^6 V$^6_5$ I

6. Complete the following tonic prolongations in four parts for SATB.

So far, you have been adding to the basic progression I–V–I. Now you are ready to create a longer chord progression by adding the tonic prolongation to a pre-dominant chord followed by a dominant chord and finally a closing tonic.

Study the following progression.

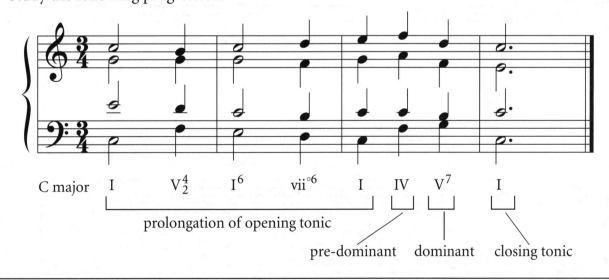

Inversions of the Dominant 7th

A V chord may be turned into a V⁷ by adding a passing tone in one of the top three voices. The figuration V⁸⁻⁷ indicates the interval of an octave (doubled root) above the bass moving to the interval of a 7th. The other notes of V⁷ are held and the dominant 7th resolves with the seventh falling a step to chord I. This passing 7th moves through scale degrees $\hat5\ \hat4\ \hat3$. Remember that figured bass symbols do not specify range—an 8 can indicate an octave or a 15th.

A passing 7th in the bass is figured V–$^4_2$. The introduction of the seventh in the bass produces the third inversion of V⁷. V$^4_2$ resolves in the usual way to I⁶.

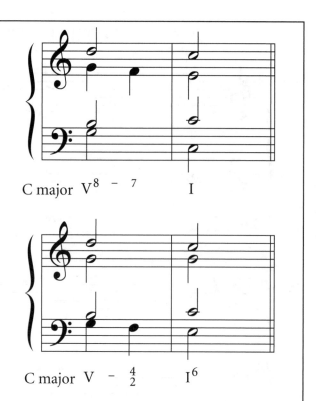

C major V⁸ – 7   I

C major V – $^4_2$ I⁶

7. Turn the following V chords into V⁷s by adding passing 7ths. Use quarter notes for the tones that move to the seventh.

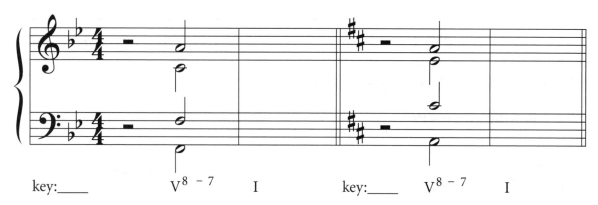

key:____   V⁸ – 7   I   key:____   V⁸ – 7   I

8. Turn the following V chords into V$^4_2$ chords and resolve them to I⁶. Use quarter notes for the tones that move to the seventh.

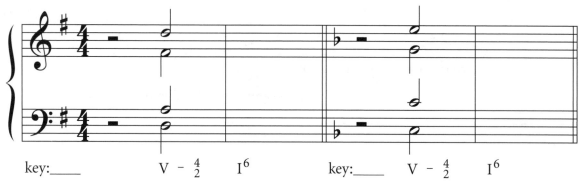

key:____   V – $^4_2$ I⁶   key:____   V – $^4_2$ I⁶

V⁷–V⁶₅: Expanding the Dominant

V⁷ and its inversions may be used to prolong the dominant area of our basic progression. In this example, V⁷ is prolonged using its first inversion. The seventh and leading note may move freely, as long as the V⁷ is prolonged. They resolve when the harmony moves to I.

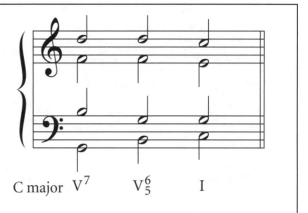

C major   V⁷   V⁶₅   I

9.   Add soprano, alto, and tenor parts to complete the following progressions.

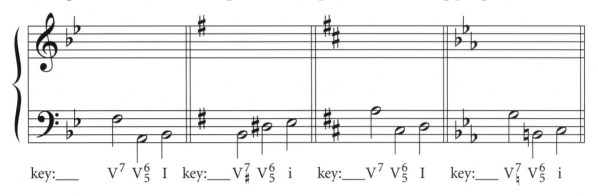

key:___   V⁷ V⁶₅ I   key:___ V⁷# V⁶₅ i   key:___ V⁷ V⁶₅ I   key:___ V⁷♮ V⁶₅ i

10.   Complete the following progressions in four parts for SATB.

(a)

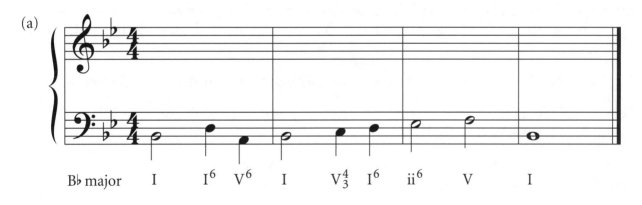

B♭ major   I   I⁶ V⁶   I   V⁴₃ I⁶   ii⁶   V   I

(b)

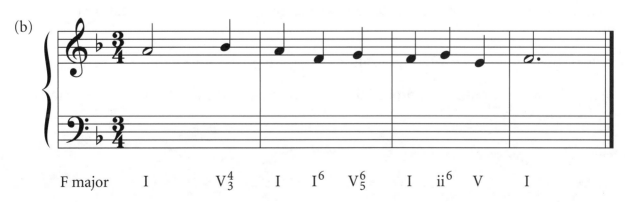

F major   I   V⁴₃   I   I⁶   V⁶₅   I   ii⁶   V   I

INVERSIONS OF THE DOMINANT 7TH

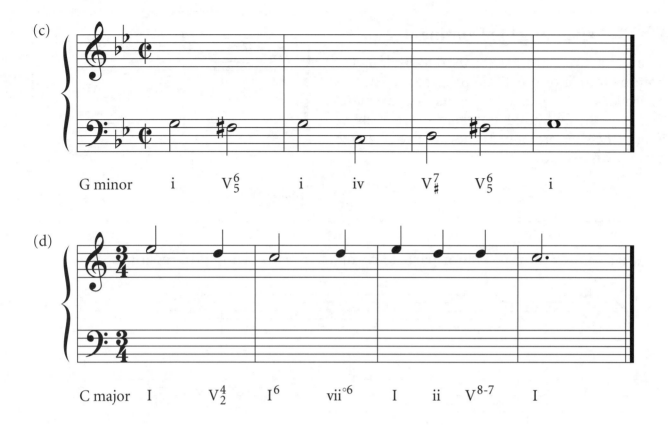

SUMMARY OF LESSON 10

1. Inversions of V^7 can be used to prolong the tonic. The root position of a dominant 7th (V^7) occurs before the closing tonic in a perfect cadence, and may also be used in the middle of a phrase.

2. Inversions of V^7 are written as complete chords with the root, third, fifth, and seventh.

3. When resolving inversions of V^7, the leading note rises ($\hat{7}$–$\hat{1}$) and the seventh falls ($\hat{4}$–$\hat{3}$). The only exception to this is V^4_3–I^6.

4. Inversions of V^7 can function as passing chords, neighbor chords, and incomplete neighbor chords between statements of I or I^6 in tonic prolongation.

5. V may be turned into V^7 with the addition of a passing 7th ($\hat{8}$–$\hat{7}$) in the soprano, alto, or tenor.

6. V may be turned into a V^4_2 with the addition of a passing 7th in the bass.

7. The dominant area of our basic progression may be expanded using V^7 and its inversions (for example, V^7–V^6_5).

LESSON 11
HARMONIC ANALYSIS 2

Appoggiaturas

An *appoggiatura* (**App**) is a non-chord tone that occurs on the strong beat or a stronger part of the beat than the note of resolution. *Appoggiaturas* are approached by leap, and left by step. They resolve to the chord tone that they replace.

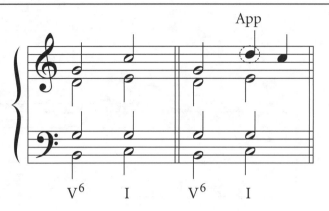

written: played:

In the 17th and 18th centuries, the *appoggiatura* was often written like a grace note, but unlike a grace note, the *appoggiatura* is played on the beat. Thus, it is an accented non-chord tone.

Anticipations

An **anticipation** (**Antic**) is a note of the next chord that appears before the rest of the chord. It is usually approached by step and left by repetition. Anticipations occur on an unaccented beat or part of a beat, and as their name implies, they anticipate the next chord tone. They occur often in a perfect cadence in the soprano voice.

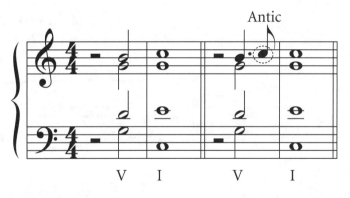

1. Provide a harmonic analysis of the following pieces using functional chord symbols. Circle and identify any non-chord tones.

Piano Concerto no. 1
op. 15 (1st movement)

(a)

Ludwig van Beethoven
(1770–1827)

key:_____

Sonatina in C major
op. 20, no. 1 (2nd movement)

(b)

Friedrich Kuhlau
(1786–1832)

key:_____

(i) Find and circle an example of a melodic sequence.

Sonatina in C major
(1st movement)

(c)

Tobias Haslinger
(1787–1842)

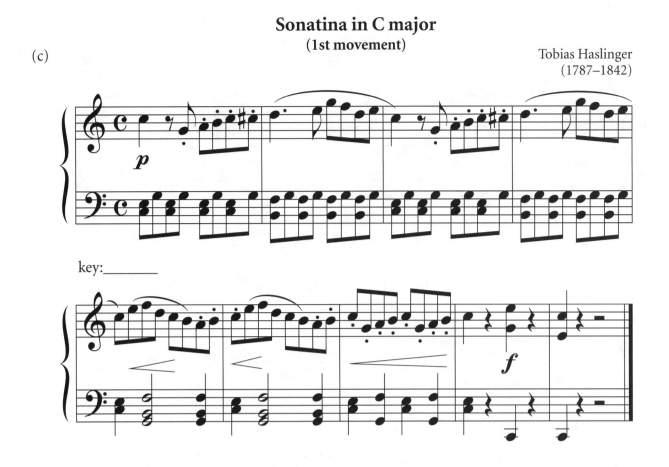

key:_____

Piano Sonata
Hob. XVI:34 (3rd movement)

(d)

Franz Joseph Haydn
(1732–1809)

key:_____

Sarabande
from **Suite in D minor, HWV 447**

(e)

George Frideric Handel
(1685–1759)

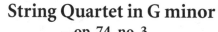

key:_____

String Quartet in G minor
op. 74, no. 3

(f)

Franz Joseph Haydn
(1732–1809)

key:_____

(i) Find and circle an example of a melodic sequence.
(ii) Find and circle one melodic diminished 5th.

LESSON 12
PROLONGING I WITH IV, ii, AND ii⁶

The pre-dominant chords IV, ii, and ii⁶ may be used before vii°⁶, V⁶, and inversions of V⁷ to prolong tonic harmony.

Here are four tonic prolongations that use pre-dominant harmony.

C major I ii V$_5^6$ I I ii V⁶ I C minor i IV♮ vii°♮⁶ i i ii°$_{♮}^6$ V♮$_2^4$ i⁶

The examples above are only a few of a variety of possible progressions using a pre-dominant chord before vii°⁶, V⁶, and inversions of V⁷ in tonic prolongation.

1. A ii chord often precedes V$_5^6$ and V⁶ (see Examples ❶ and ❷).

2. In Example ❸, the progression i–IV♮–vii°♮⁶–i supports a rising soprano line consisting of scale degrees $\hat{5}\,\hat{6}\,\hat{7}\,\hat{1}$. This same soprano line can support the progression i–IV♮–vii°♮⁶–i⁶. The use of the melodic minor scale (with A natural) avoids a melodic augmented 2nd in the soprano.

3. A ii°$_{♮}^6$ chord works well before V♮$_2^4$ in tonic prolongation, as illustrated in Example ❹. The repetition of a bass note from a weak beat to a strong beat is acceptable when the second note is dissonant (here, it is the seventh). Tension increases rather than decreases with this repetition. IV is another good choice to precede V♮$_2^4$. Remember that V♮$_2^4$ resolves to i⁶. The melodic minor scale avoids a melodic augmented 2nd in the tenor (A natural). This is required when a rising line involving $\hat{6}$ and $\hat{7}$ is desired. Whenever possible, ♭$\hat{6}$ may be used by keeping it in a different voice than ♯$\hat{7}$.

4. When a pre-dominant chord precedes an inversion of V⁷, the seventh is normally prepared by being held over as a common tone. When writing the bass line for these progressions, be careful to avoid awkward leaps and melodic augmented intervals.

1. Write functional chord symbols to analyze the following progressions.

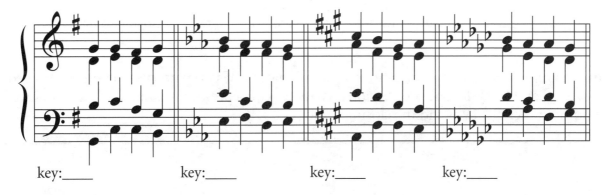

key:___   key:___   key:___   key:___

PROLONGING I WITH IV, ii, AND ii⁶

2. Complete the following figured basses in four parts for SATB. (Notes without figures indicate root-position chords.)

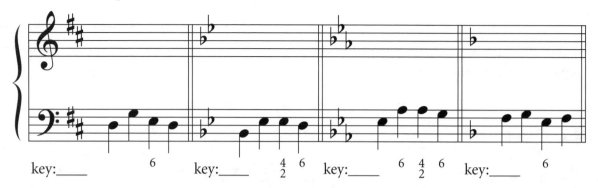

key:____   6   key:____   4 6   key:____   6 4 6   key:____   6
                           2   2

3. Add functional chord symbols and alto and tenor parts to complete the following tonic prolongations.

key:____   key:____   key:____   key:____

Tonic prolongations using chords IV, ii, and ii⁶ can be used in conjunction with other tonic prolongation patterns to produce longer progressions.

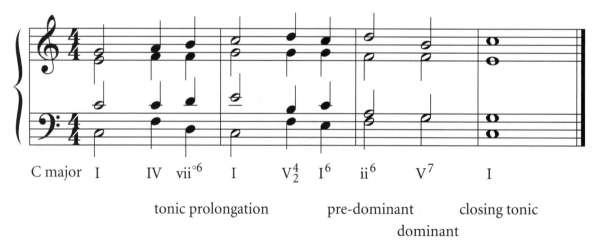

C major   I   IV vii°⁶   I   V⁴₂ I⁶   ii⁶   V⁷   I

            tonic prolongation   pre-dominant   closing tonic
                                         dominant

In this example, the tonic prolongation is a combination of two patterns previously learned: I–IV–vii°⁶–I and I–V⁴₂–I⁶. The progression concludes with a pre-dominant chord (ii⁶), followed by a dominant chord (V⁷) and the closing tonic (I).

---

4.   Harmonize the following figured bass in four parts for SATB.

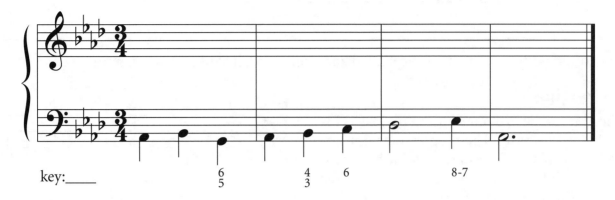

5.   Complete the following in four parts for SATB.

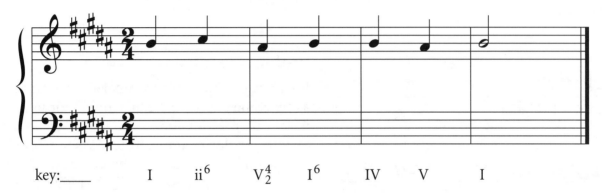

SUMMARY OF LESSON 12

1.   The pre-dominant chords IV, ii, and ii[6] may precede vii[6], V[6], and inversions of V[7] in tonic prolongation.

2.   These progressions may be joined to other tonic prolongations to produce longer progressions.

3.   When a pre-dominant chord precedes an inversion of V[7], the seventh is normally prepared by keeping the common tone in the same voice.

4.   Use of the melodic form of the minor scale (raised 6th degree) will avoid the interval of a melodic augmented 2nd. This is required when a rising line involving $\hat{6}$ and $\hat{7}$ is desired. Whenever possible, $\flat\hat{6}$ may be used by keeping it in a different voice than $\sharp\hat{7}$.

LESSON 13
PROLONGING THE PRE-DOMINANT

Pre-dominant harmony can be expanded and prolonged, just like tonic harmony.

Prolonging ii

Chord ii can be prolonged using ii^6, just as I is prolonged using I^6. The progressions ii–ii^6 or ii^6–ii are prolongations of supertonic harmony. One of the easiest ways to write this progression is to use voice exchange between the soprano and bass. Doubling may vary; here, the third is doubled in ii^6, and the alto and tenor must leap in order to avoid parallel octaves.

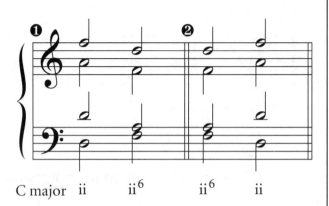

C major   ii   ii^6 ii^6 ii

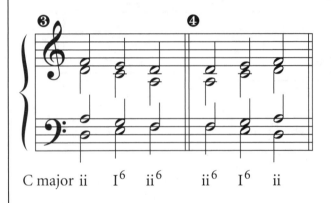

C major ii   I^6 ii^6 ii^6 I^6 ii

Prolonging ii Using I^6

I^6 can be used to prolong supertonic harmony as a passing chord between ii and ii^6, or ii^6 and ii. In this progression, I^6 does not act as an opening or closing tonic. Instead, its function is to prolong ii. Because of the voice exchange between soprano and bass (DEF–FED), I^6 has a doubled third.

Parallel 5ths can be a problem with the progressions ii–I^6–ii^6 and ii^6–I^6–ii. Faulty parallels can be avoided in two ways.

1. Write the progressions in close position with the voices as close together as possible (see Examples ❸ and ❹).

2. Double the third in chord ii, instead of the root (as in Examples ❻ and ❼).

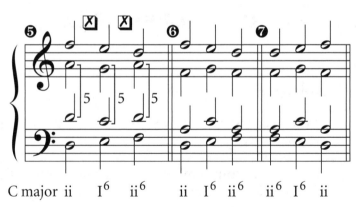

C major ii   I^6 ii^6 ii   I^6 ii^6 ii^6 I^6 ii

1. Add functional chord symbols and alto and tenor parts to complete the following supertonic prolongations.

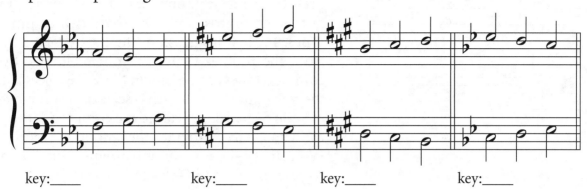

key:____   key:____   key:____   key:____

2. Complete the following progression for SATB.

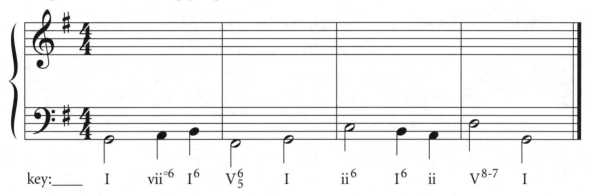

key:____   I   vii°⁶   I⁶   V⁶₅   I   ii⁶   I⁶   ii   V⁸⁻⁷   I

Prolonging the Pre-dominant with IV–ii⁶

Pre-dominant harmony can be prolonged with the progression IV–ii⁶. IV and ii⁶ share two common tones. Since the third of ii⁶ is doubled, it is only necessary to change one note of IV to make a ii⁶ chord.

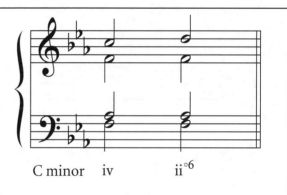

C minor   iv   ii°⁶

3. Add soprano, alto, and tenor voices to complete the following progression.

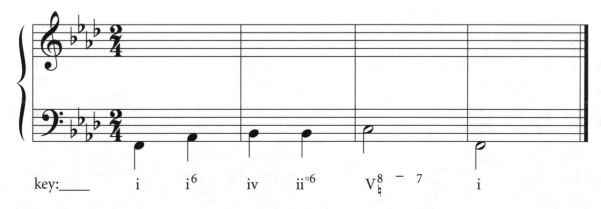

key:____   i   i⁶   iv   ii°⁶   V⁸♮ − 7   i

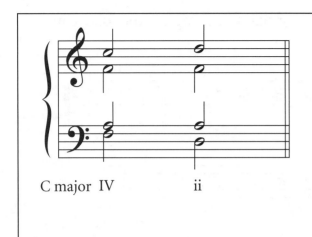

C major IV   ii

The progression IV–ii is also a prolongation of pre-dominant harmony. Both IV and ii are pre-dominant chords, and they share two common tones. In this progression, the bass drops a 3rd from the root of IV to the root of ii. The two common tones can be kept in the same voices, and the remaining voice, which is scale degree $\hat{1}$, moves to scale degree $\hat{2}$. Repeating the common tones in the same voices provides the smoothest motion. IV–ii and IV–ii⁶ are common progressions, but the reverse (ii–IV and ii⁶–IV) are not often used.

4. Complete the following progressions in four parts for SATB.

(a)

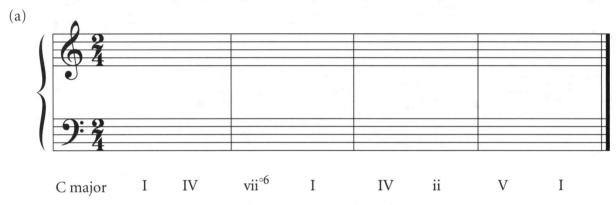

C major   I   IV   vii°⁶   I   IV   ii   V   I

(b)

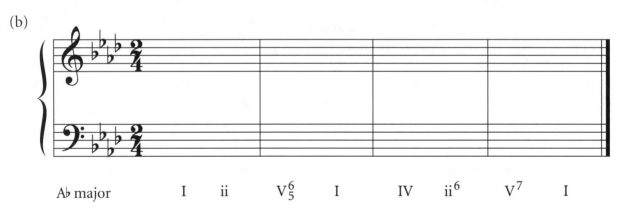

A♭ major   I   ii   V⁶₅   I   IV   ii⁶   V⁷   I

(c)

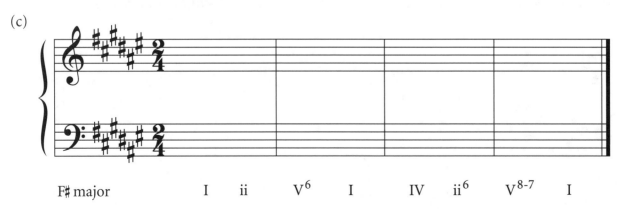

F♯ major   I   ii   V⁶   I   IV   ii⁶   V⁸⁻⁷   I

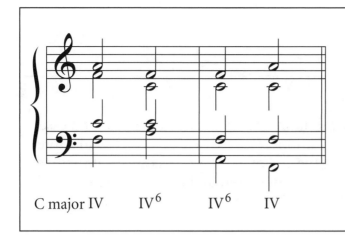

Prolonging IV with IV⁶

The pre-dominant IV can be prolonged with IV⁶. One of the easiest ways to write this progression is to use voice exchange between the soprano and bass. In the progression IV–IV⁶, the fifth of IV⁶ is doubled, but other options are possible. In the progression IV⁶–IV, keeping two common tones in the same voices provides the smoothest motion.

C major IV   IV⁶   IV⁶   IV

5. Complete the following progressions in four parts for SATB.

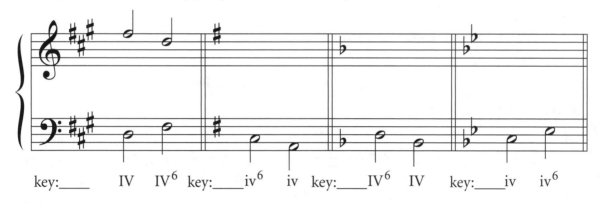

key:____   IV   IV⁶ key:____ iv⁶   iv   key:____ IV⁶   IV   key:____ iv   iv⁶

6. Add alto and tenor voices to complete the following progression.

key:____   I   IV⁶   IV   V⁷   I

7. Provide a harmonic analysis of the following progression using functional chord symbols.

key:____

LESSON 14
CHORD vi

Substituting vi for I

Chord vi can be used as a substitute for the closing tonic in a harmonic progression. In this case, V or V[7] resolves to vi instead of I. This resolution is called a **deceptive resolution**. When the progression V–vi occurs as a cadence at the end of a phrase, it is called a **deceptive cadence**. This cadence can be used at the end of a phrase, but rarely at the end of a piece. Chord vi provides a strong contrast to I in its resolution to V. In major keys, vi is a minor chord, whereas I is major. In minor keys, VI is major and i is minor.

The bass approach to vi is different than the approach to chord I. V[7] must be a complete chord to resolve to vi. The resolution of V[7] to vi is much like that of V[7] to I.

1.	The leading note ($\hat{7}$) rises to the tonic ($\hat{1}$).

2.	The seventh of V[7] ($\hat{4}$) resolves downward to $\hat{3}$.

3.	Scale degree $\hat{2}$ moves to $\hat{1}$.

4.	The bass moves to the root of vi (rather than the root of I).

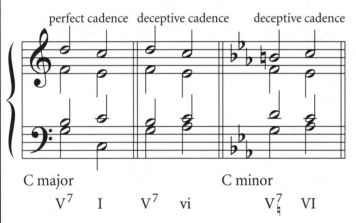

The third of vi is doubled when vi is a substitute for I. In this progression (V[7]–vi), the bass and the leading note rise, and the other two voices fall. In minor keys, the leading note ($\hat{7}$) must resolve to $\hat{1}$. If it drops, a melodic augmented 2nd will occur.

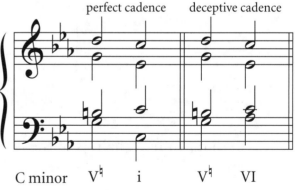

The resolution of V to vi is similar to that of V[7] to vi. The only difference is that scale degree $\hat{5}$ (which is the doubled root of chord V) moves down a 3rd to scale degree $\hat{3}$ in chord vi. The third is doubled in vi, and two voices rise while two voices fall in the move from V to vi.

In the deceptive resolution, it is important to follow the voice leading procedures on this page to avoid faulty parallels.

1. Complete the following deceptive resolutions of V⁷ and V.

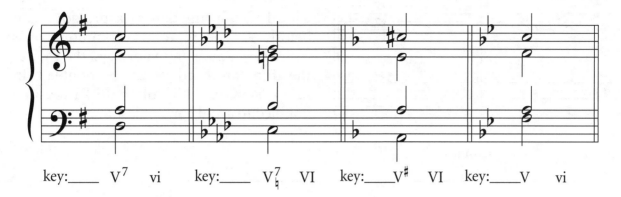

key:____ V^7 vi   key:____ V$^7_{\natural}$ VI   key:____V$^{\sharp}$ VI   key:____V vi

2. Write the following deceptive resolutions of V and V⁷.

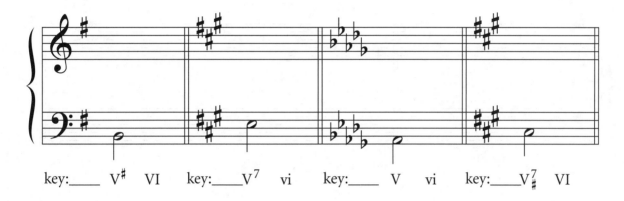

key:____ V$^{\sharp}$ VI   key:____V^7 vi   key:____ V vi   key:____V$^7_{\sharp}$ VI

3. Complete the following figured bass patterns for SATB.

(a)

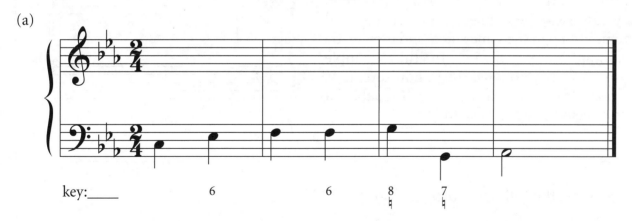

key:____   6   6   8♮   7♮

(b)

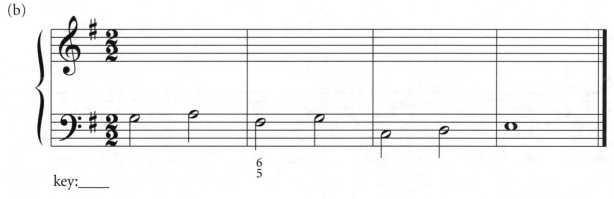

key:____   6 5

Chord vi

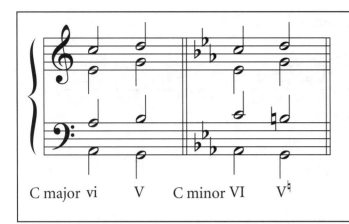

Using vi as a Pre-dominant

Chord vi can function as a pre-dominant before V. There are no common tones between vi and V. In major keys, the root or the third of chord vi can be doubled. In minor keys, the third of chord VI must be doubled to avoid a melodic augmented 2nd.

C major vi   V   C minor VI   V♮

4. Complete the following progressions. (Make note of the soprano lines in these progressions.)

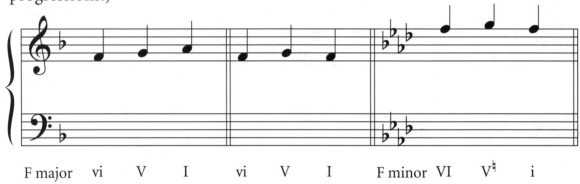

F major vi V I vi V I   F minor VI V♮ i

I–vi

Chords I and vi share two common tones. They can easily be connected by keeping both common tones in the same voices and moving the remaining voice stepwise. In this example, the root of vi is doubled. In minor keys, if VI progresses to V, the third of VI must be doubled to avoid a melodic augmented 2nd.

C major I   vi

5. Complete the following progressions for SATB.

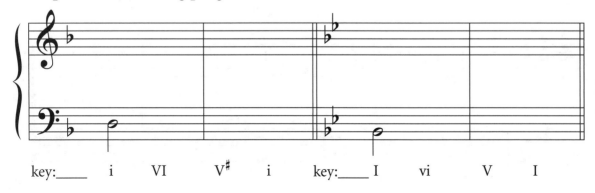

key:____ i VI V♯ i   key:____ I vi V I

Using vi in a Bass that Descends in 3rds

Chord vi can be used in a bass line of descending 3rds. In this case, vi occurs before IV or ii⁶, and acts as a link between the tonic and the pre-dominant.

$$I–vi–IV–V^{(7)}–I$$

or

$$I–vi–ii^6–V^{(7)}–I$$

Study the following progressions using vi in a descending-3rd bass line.

C major   I   vi   IV   V   I

I–vi–IV–V–I or i–VI–iv–V–i

In this progression, there are two common tones between I and vi, and two common tones between vi and IV. The smoothest connection is to keep the common tones in the same voices, and move the remaining voice by step. Double the root of vi.

i–VI–ii⁶–V–I or i–VI–ii°⁶–V♮–i

In this progression, there are two common tones between i and VI, and one common tone between VI and ii°⁶. The smoothest connection is to keep the common tones in the same voices, and move the remaining voices by step. Double the root of VI and the root or third of ii°⁶. It is fine to double the root of VI here in a minor key because the following chord is not V so augmented 2nds are not a possibility.

C minor   i   VI   ii°⁶   V♮   i

6.   Complete the following progressions using a descending-3rd bass line.

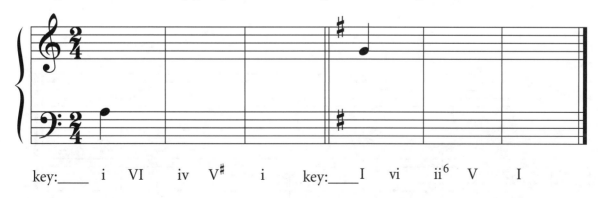

key:____   i   VI   iv   V♯   i   key:____   I   vi   ii⁶   V   I

Chord vi

C major I vi ii V⁷ I

Chord vi can also lead to ii. In this case, the bass either falls a 5th or rises a 4th. There is one common tone between vi and ii, so the smoothest voice-leading is common-tone stepwise motion. In this and in the previous progressions, the function of vi is to act as a link between the tonic and the pre-dominant. Since ii is not used in root position in minor keys, this progression is used in major keys only.

7. Complete the following progressions in four parts for SATB.

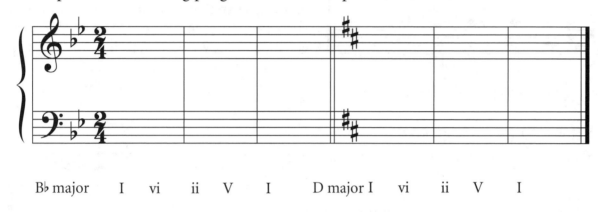

Bb major I vi ii V I   D major I vi ii V I

8. Add soprano, alto, and tenor parts to complete the following figured bass lines.

(a)

key:____   6   8 – 7

(b)

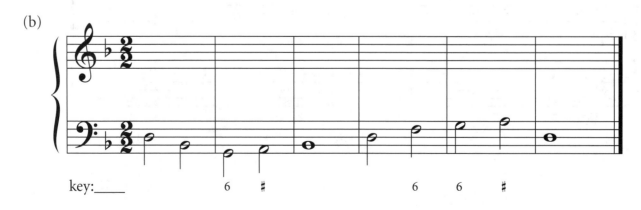

key:____   6   ♯   6   6   ♯

(c)

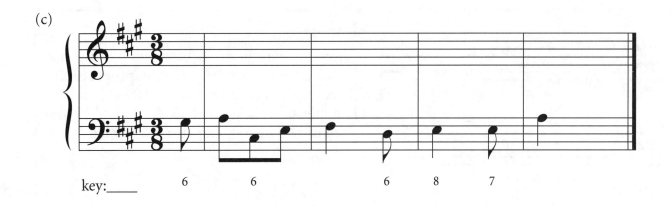

key:____   6   6   6   8   7

9. Provide an analysis of the following examples using functional chord symbols. Circle and identify any non-chord tones.

(a)

key:____

(b)

key:____

(c)

key:____

Chord vi

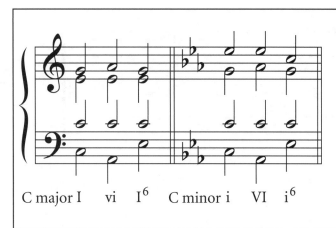

C major I   vi   I⁶   C minor i   VI   i⁶

I–vi–I⁶

Chord vi may be used between I and I⁶ to prolong tonic harmony. In this progression, there are two common tones between I and vi. For the smoothest voice-leading, double the third of I⁶. The root can also be doubled.

10. Complete the following progression for SATB.

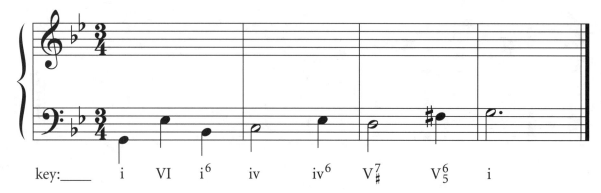

key:____   i   VI   i⁶   iv   iv⁶   V⁷#   V⁶₅   i

SUMMARY OF LESSON 14

1. A deceptive resolution occurs when vi acts as a temporary substitute for I in a closing tonic. When this progression replaces a perfect cadence, it is called a deceptive cadence.
   This progression rarely occurs at the end of a piece. Another harmonic progression usually follows.

2. V⁷ resolves to vi in much the same way that it resolves to I, with the leading note rising and the seventh falling. V⁷ must be a complete chord when it leads to vi.

3. The third of vi is doubled when it acts as a substitute for I.

4. Chord vi can act as a pre-dominant. In this case, it leads directly to V.

5. In the progression vi–V, double the third in vi. This is optional in major keys, but is essential in minor keys.

6. Chord vi can link the tonic and the pre-dominant in a series of descending 3rds in the bass (for example, I–vi–IV–V–I, or I–vi–ii⁶–V–I).

7. Chord vi may also act to link the tonic and the pre-dominant in a sequence of descending 5ths in major keys (for example, I–vi–ii–V⁽⁷⁾–I).

8. Chord vi can prolong tonic harmony when it occurs between I and I⁶.

HARMONIC ANALYSIS 3

Suspensions

A **suspension** (**Susp**) is a non-chord tone. Suspensions are notes that are held over from a previous chord (prepared), and thus delay the harmony note. They resolve by a step, usually downward. A suspension acts much like an *appoggiatura* in that it delays the appearance of the note to which it resolves. The note that prepares a suspension may be the same value or longer than the suspension note, but it usually is not shorter. Suspensions are usually tied, but they can occur without a tie as well.

A suspension consists of three elements:

(1) Preparation

The preparation starts as note of the previous chord.

(2) Suspension

The prepared note is held while the other notes move to the notes of the next chord, and it becomes dissonant to that chord.
(Note that suspensions usually occur on strong beats.)

(3) Resolution

The resolution usually occurs on a weak beat. It moves by step to a chord tone.

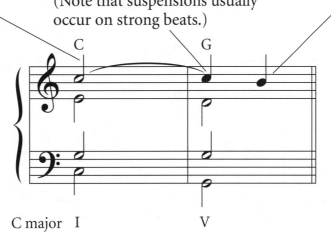

A suspension can occur in any voice. Notice that not all suspensions are tied.

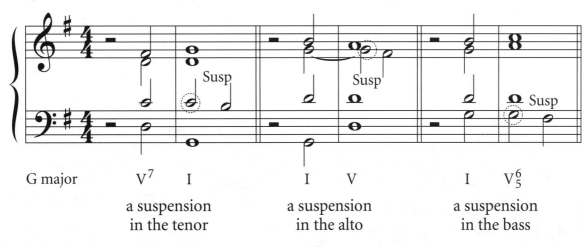

When a composer inserts one or more notes between the suspension and its resolution note, it is called an **ornamental resolution**. These extra notes must also be analyzed. They give the line more shape and make the rhythm more interesting.

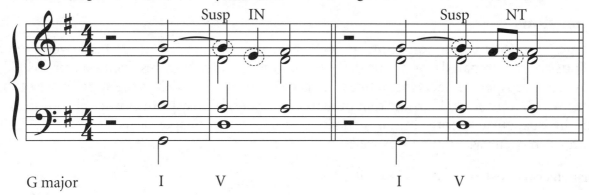

The more common suspensions are usually resolved over a held bass note. Usually they have figured bass numbers such as 9–8, 7–6, or 4–3.

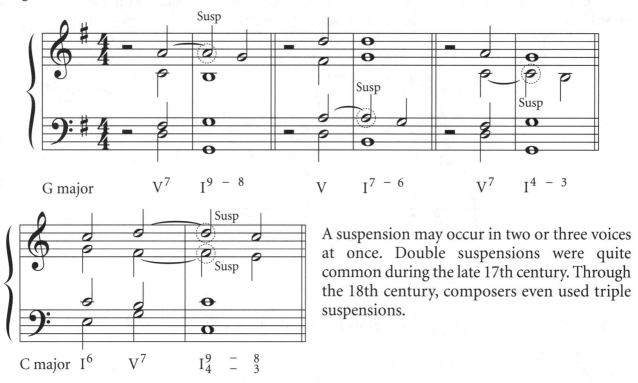

A suspension may occur in two or three voices at once. Double suspensions were quite common during the late 17th century. Through the 18th century, composers even used triple suspensions.

When several notes appear between a suspension and its resolution, the actual resolution may appear an octave lower than the preparation and suspension.

1. For the following examples, provide functional chord symbols, and circle and label the suspensions.

key:____

key:____

2. Complete the following progressions with suspensions as indicated.

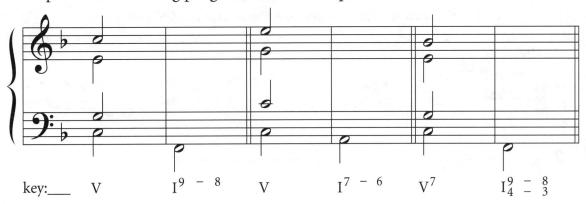

key:___ V   I$^{9-8}$ V   I$^{7-6}$ V^7 I$^9_4$ $^{-}$ $^8_3$

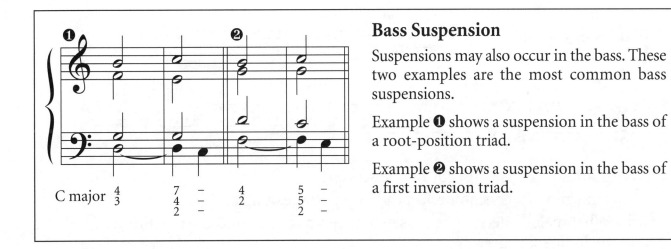

Bass Suspension

Suspensions may also occur in the bass. These two examples are the most common bass suspensions.

Example ❶ shows a suspension in the bass of a root-position triad.

Example ❷ shows a suspension in the bass of a first inversion triad.

1. Provide a functional and root/quality analysis of the following excerpts. Circle and identify any non-chord tones.

Étude
op. 47, no. 1

(a)

Stephen Heller
(1813–1888)

key:___

(i) How many suspensions occur in this excerpt? _____

Sonata in C major
no. 1 of 6 Sonatines pour clavecin ou pianoforte (2nd movement)

(b)

Johann Baptist Vaňhal
(1739–1813)

key:___

(i) Mark the phrases directly on the score.
(ii) Find and label one imperfect cadence in this example.
(iii) What melodic technique is used between phrases 1 and 2—repetition or melodic sequence? _____

Divertimento in D major
Hob. XVI:4 (Menuetto)

Franz Joseph Haydn
(1732–1809)

(c)

key:___

(i)   Mark the phrases of this excerpt directly on the score.

(ii) Name and label the cadences at the end of each phrase.

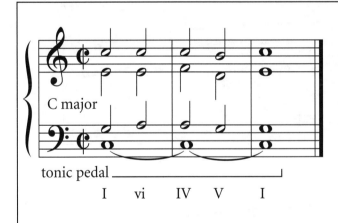

C major

tonic pedal _____

I   vi   IV   V   I

Pedal Point

A pedal point is a note that is sustained through several changes of harmony. It may or may not be part of the harmonies that are produced by the other voices. It most often occurs in the bass, but can appear in any part. A pedal point may be any note, but is usually the tonic or dominant. This non-chord tone gets its name from the organist's technique of sustaining a single tone with the pedal while playing other harmonies above it. Notice that the inversions are not indicated in the harmonic analysis. The sound of the inversions is altered by the pedal, and there are no conventional symbols to show this alteration when the pedal is in the bass. Inversions should be indicated if the pedal is in an upper voice.

The following example illustrates a double pedal that involves both the tonic and the dominant.

Schnitter liedchen (Song of the Reaper)
from **Album für die Jugend, op. 68, no. 18**

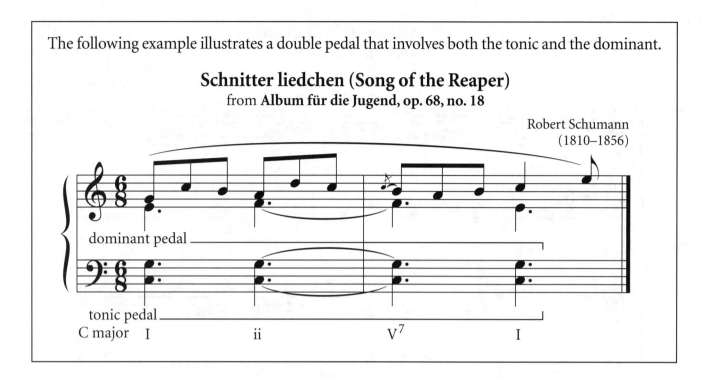

Robert Schumann
(1810–1856)

1. Analyze the following musical excerpts. Name the key, provide functional chord symbols, and circle and identify any non-chord tones.

German Dance no. 10
from **12 Deutsche Tänze, Hob. IX: 12**

(a)

Franz Joseph Haydn
(1732–1809)

Nina's Aria "Il mio ben quando verrà"
from *Nina,* act 1, scene 6

(b)

Giovanni Paisiello
(1740–1816)

key:___

Chorale no. 22: Schmücke dich, o liebe Seele
from **341 Four-Part Chorales**

(c)

Johann Sebastian Bach
(1685–1750)

key:___

LESSON 16
MELODIC FIGURATION

Four-part writing consists of two basic elements.

Melody: The horizontal aspect of the music. The shape of each melodic line, the chord progressions, and the relationship between the different parts.

Harmony: The vertical aspect of the music. The chords that we use, and the spacing of the notes in these chords.

These two elements are of equal importance in good writing.

Melodic figuration—the addition of non-chord tones such as passing tones or neighbor tones—is an important part of musical composition. These added notes play an extremely important role in music. Even though they are ornamental, their function is much more than just decoration.

The notes of figuration are:

Passing tones	Changing notes
Accented passing tones	Appoggiaturas
Neighbor tones	Anticipations
Accented neighbor tones	Suspensions
Incomplete neighbor tones	Chordal skips

B♭ major   I   I⁶   ii   ii⁶   V

A **chordal skip** is a harmony note that occurs on a weak beat or weak part of the beat. It can break up large leaps, change the position of a chord, and aid in preventing parallel 5ths and octaves.

The chart on the following two pages lists non-chord tones and their use in melodic figuration.

Non-chord tone	Approached	Left	Metrical position	Use in melodic figuration
Passing tone (PT) C major I I⁶	by step	by step	weak	skip between two notes
Accented passing tone (APT) C major I I⁶	by step	by step	strong	skip between two notes
Upper neighbor tone (NT) C major I⁶ I	by step	by step	weak	between two common notes
Lower neighbor tone (NT) C major I⁶ I	by step	by step	weak	between two common notes
Accented neighbor (ANT) C major I I⁶	by step	by step	strong	between two common notes
Incomplete neighbor (INT) C major I vi⁶ C major vi⁶ V⁶	by leap	by step	weak	stepwise motion up stepwise motion down

MELODIC FIGURATION

Non-chord tone	Approached	Left	Metrical position	Use in melodic figuration
Échappée (Ech) C major I V C major I V⁷	by step	by leap	weak	stepwise motion down stepwise motion up
Changing notes (CN) C major I⁶	by step or leap	by step or leap	variable	between two common tones
Anticipation (Antic) C major vii°⁶ I C major V I	by step (usually)	by repeat	weak	stepwise up (e.g., $\hat{7}$ to $\hat{1}$) stepwise down (e.g., $\hat{2}$ to $\hat{1}$)
Suspension (Susp) C major I⁶ vii°⁶	by same note	by step	strong	stepwise motion down sometimes up (e.g., 7–8 susp.)
Appoggiatura (App) C major I V	by leap	by step	strong	leap

Here is a simple harmonization in C major.

C major

Here is the same harmonization with the addition of suspensions, passing tones, and neighbor tones. The addition of these non-chord tones adds rhythmic interest and motion. They also give the music a richer and more expressive texture.

C major

1. For the following progressions, name the key and symbolize the chords using functional chord symbols. Rewrite them, adding non-chord tones where appropriate. Observe correct voice-leading and be careful to avoid faulty parallels.

(a)

key:_____

Melodic Figuration

(b)

key:_____

(c)

key:_____

LESSON 17
CHORD iii

Chord iii is used relatively rarely. In major keys, chord iii is minor. It can be used between I and IV to support a descending soprano line of scale degrees $\hat{1}$–$\hat{7}$–$\hat{6}$. The usual rule is that the leading note rises in the soprano or bass, but if $\hat{7}$ is part of a descending line, it does not resolve to $\hat{1}$. When scale degree $\hat{7}$ ascends to $\hat{1}$, it is harmonized with a dominant chord or vii°6. However, when scale degree $\hat{7}$ descends to scale degree $\hat{6}$, it is often harmonized with iii.

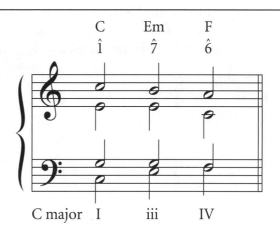

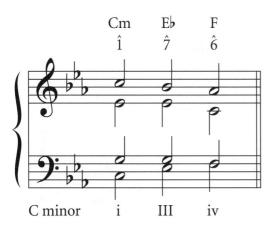

I–iii

It is best to double the root of chord iii. There are two common tones between I and iii. The smoothest connection is to repeat the common tones in the same voices and move the remaining voice (soprano) by step.

In minor keys, the progression i–III–iv uses the descending melodic minor scale, in which the leading note is not raised, thus preventing a melodic augmented 2nd that would occur between $\hat{7}$ and $\hat{6}$ in the descending line $\hat{1}$–$\hat{7}$–$\hat{6}$. Here, the distance between $\hat{1}$ and $\hat{7}$ is a whole tone. The term "leading note" is used for scale degree $\hat{7}$ only when it is a semitone away from $\hat{1}$. Since $\hat{7}$ does not function as a leading note, it is referred to as the **subtonic**. Chord III is major in this progression.

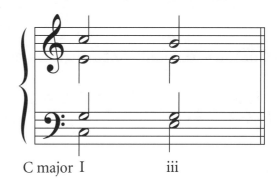

iii–IV

There are no common tones between iii and IV. The smoothest connection, which avoids faulty parallels, is made by moving the three upper notes in contrary motion to the bass to the nearest available chord tones.

CHORD iii

The progression I–iii–IV can proceed in two ways:

1. The IV following iii can act as a pre-dominant, leading to a dominant chord followed by a closing tonic. Here, iii acts as a link between the tonic and the predominant. In this example in C minor, $\hat{7}$ is not raised in chord III, but must be raised in chord V at the cadence, where it functions as a leading note.

C minor   i   III   iv   V♮   i

2. The progression I–iii–IV may be followed by I or I⁶, thus prolonging tonic harmony.

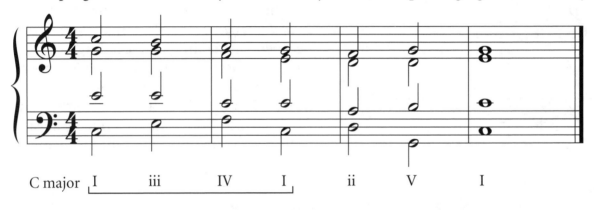

C major   I   iii   IV   I   ii   V   I

1. Complete the following progressions in four parts for SATB.

(a)

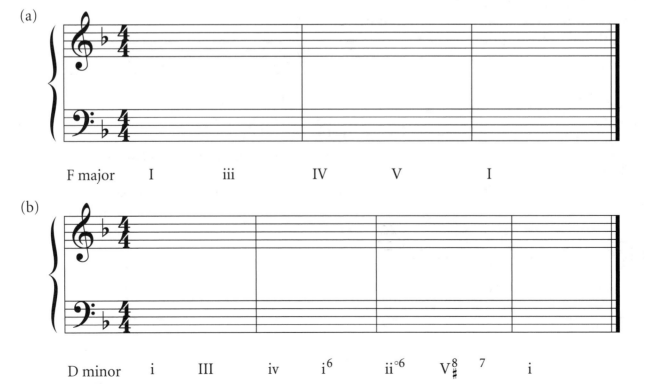

F major   I   iii   IV   V   I

(b)

D minor   i   III   iv   i⁶   ii°⁶   V$^{8\quad 7}_{\sharp}$ i

2. Provide a harmonic analysis of the following progressions using functional chord symbols.

(a)

key:_____

(b)

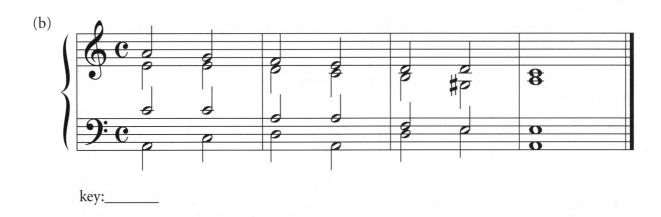

key:_____

SUMMARY OF LESSON 17

1. Chord iii is a minor chord in major keys, and may be used between I and IV to support a descending soprano line using scale tones $\hat{1}$, $\hat{7}$, and $\hat{6}$.

2. In minor keys, scale degree $\hat{7}$ is not raised in chord III, so as to avoid a melodic augmented 2nd between raised $\hat{7}$ and $\hat{6}$. Here, III is a major chord. Double the root of chord III in this progression.

3. There are two common tones between I and iii. Keep the common tones in the same voices and move the remaining voice (soprano) down by step.

4. There are no common tones between iii and IV. Move the upper voices in contrary motion to the bass to the nearest available chord tones.

5. The progression I–iii–IV can lead to dominant harmony followed by the closing tonic.

6. The progression I–iii–IV can be followed by I or I⁶, in which case it functions as a tonic prolongation.

Lesson 18
Sequences

In major keys, vii° is a diminished chord and is most often used in first inversion. Chord vii° in root position can be used in a series of root-position chords descending in 5ths, as shown in the example below. This pattern is called a **sequence**. The bass alternates descending 5ths and ascending 4ths. Notice that the voice-leading patterns in each voice maintain the same motion throughout: the soprano steps up, the alto holds a common tone, the tenor steps up. The voice-leading in the three upper parts alternates at every second chord, just as the direction of the bass changes. It is important to follow this voice-leading, since a sequence is based on the repetition of different patterns of scale degrees in melodic lines.

In this progression, vii° leads to iii. The root of each chord is doubled. This leads to a doubled leading note in chord vii°, which is allowed since vii° does not move to I and the leading note does not resolve to scale degree 1̂. Note the use of chord iii in this progression. It occurs between vii and vi in the series of descending 5ths. Here, the melodic augmented 4th that occurs in the bass between IV and vii° is correct.

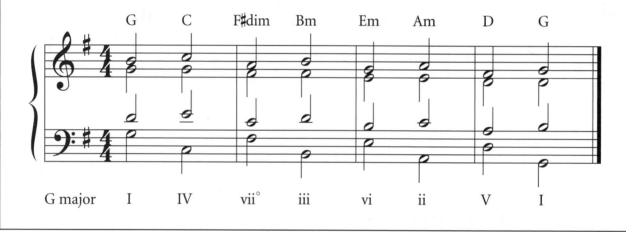

1. Complete the following progression for SATB.

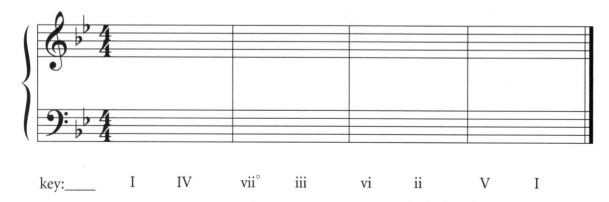

2. Harmonize the following melody in four parts using a series of descending 5ths.

F major

The descending-5ths sequence can also be written in minor keys. Scale degree $\hat{7}$ is not raised in chords VII and III since it does not function as a leading note. In chord V, however, $\hat{7}$ is raised for the perfect cadence at the end of the sequence. VII and III are major chords in this progression. Chord ii, a diminished chord that is rarely used in root position in minor keys, is also found in this progression.

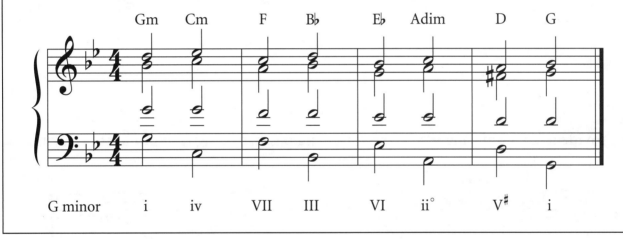

SEQUENCES

3. Harmonize the following progressions in four parts using a series of descending 5ths.

(a)

C minor

(b)

E minor

4. Provide a harmonic analysis of the following passage using functional chord symbols.

key:___

The descending-5ths sequence does not always occur with the chords in root position. In the two variations of the progression given below, every second chord is written in first inversion. The sequential pattern in each voice is maintained throughout until the final root-position I of the perfect cadence. These progressions are effective in major and minor keys. In minor keys, $\hat{7}$ is not raised in chords VII and III, since its goal is not $\hat{1}$, but $\hat{7}$ is raised in V where it functions as the leading note. These examples contain complete sequences, but it is not necessary to complete the series of descending 5ths. Shorter segments of sequences are also quite useful.

5. Complete the following sequence by adding soprano, alto, and tenor voices.

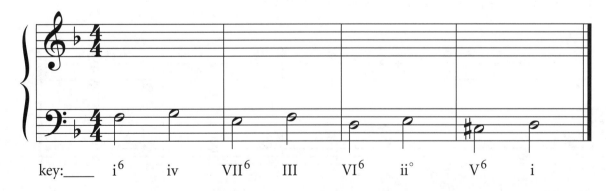

A common sequence occurs in the well-known *Canon in D major* by Johann Pachelbel. In Pachelbel's Canon, the sequential chords are in root position (I–V–vi–iii–IV–I). Notice that the leading note ($\hat{7}$), which occurs in chord V, descends to the doubled root of chord vi instead of rising to the tonic ($\hat{1}$). This voice-leading is necessary to keep the sequential motion of the voices consistent.

Johann Pachelbel
(1653–1706)

D major   I   V   vi   iii   IV   I   IV   V

To write this sequence in minor keys, the minor v chord must not have a raised leading note so as to avoid a melodic augmented 2nd. If a raised leading note is used, the leading note must resolve upward. This will interrupt the downward motion of the sequence.

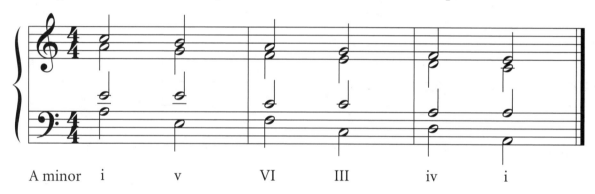

A minor   i   v   VI   III   iv   i

This progression is also effective with first-inversion chords (I–V⁶–vi–iii⁶–IV–I⁶) and can be used to harmonize a descending scale in the bass. The sequence ends with the I⁶ chord, and can be completed with a perfect cadence using vii⁶–I or V$_3^4$–I.

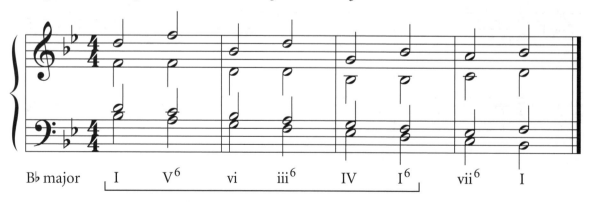

B♭ major   I   V⁶   vi   iii⁶   IV   I⁶   vii⁶   I

6. Add soprano, alto, and tenor voices to complete the following sequence.

key:____   I   V   vi   iii   IV   I

7. Complete the following sequence.

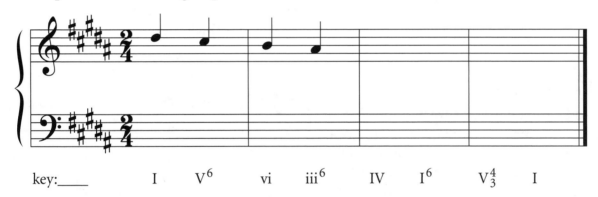

key:____   I   V⁶   vi   iii⁶   IV   I⁶   V₃⁴   I

SUMMARY OF LESSON 18

1. Chord viiº is a diminished chord and is usually used in first inversion.

2. Chord viiº can be used in root position in a sequence consisting of descending 5ths: I–IV–viiº–iii–vi–ii–V–I. In this progression, the root of each chord is doubled. This results in a doubled leading note in chord viiº, which is acceptable because viiº does not move to I, and the leading note ($\hat{7}$) does not resolve to $\hat{1}$.

3. A sequence is a repetition of a melodic or harmonic pattern at a higher or lower pitch.

4. One common sequence is the "Pachelbel Canon" sequence: I–V–vi–iii–IV–I.

5. The chords in these sequences do not have to be used in root position. Variations using first inversion chords are also effective.

Lesson 19
Chord IV in Tonic Prolongation

Chord IV usually functions as a pre-dominant chord, but it may also be used to prolong tonic harmony.

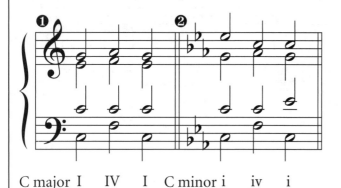

C major   I   IV   I   C minor   i   iv   i

I–IV–I

Chord IV can prolong tonic harmony when it occurs between two statements of I. For the smoothest voice-leading, keep the common tone in the same voice and move the other voices in neighbor motion. Other voice-leading is also possible. Examples ❶ and ❷ show two different voice-leading options for this progression.

I–IV–I⁶ and I⁶–IV–I⁶

Chord IV can be used between statements of I and I⁶ or two statements of I⁶ in tonic prolongation. When I⁶ comes before or after IV, it is best to double the root in IV and the fifth in I⁶. This results in the smoothest voice-leading and helps to avoid faulty parallels.

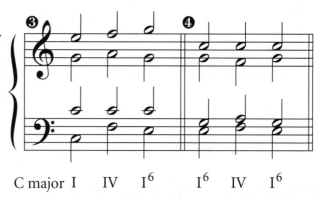

C major   I   IV   I⁶   I⁶   IV   I⁶

IV⁶ in Tonic Prolongation

Chord IV⁶ can be used in the progression I–IV⁶–I⁶ to prolong tonic harmony. The bass line descends, and the most common soprano line for this progression is $\hat{3}$ $\hat{4}$ $\hat{5}$. For the smoothest voice-leading, keep the common tone in the same voice and double the third in IV⁶ and the fifth in I⁶.

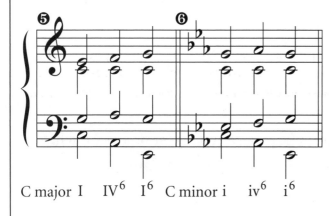

C major   I   IV⁶   I⁶   C minor   i   iv⁶   i⁶

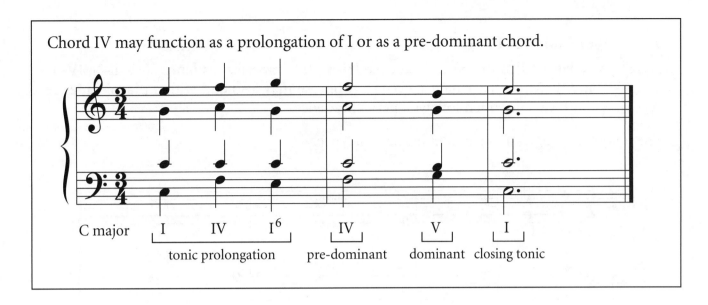

Chord IV may function as a prolongation of I or as a pre-dominant chord.

1. Set the following figured bass in four parts.

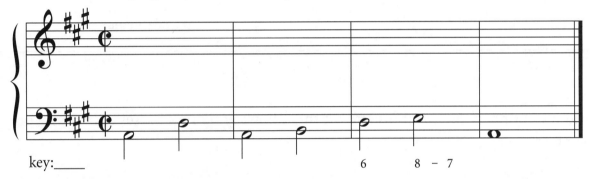

key:___

6   8 – 7

2. Add functional chord symbols, and harmonize the following melodies using IV in tonic prolongation.

(a)

B♭ major

(b)

G minor

The Plagal Cadence IV–I

So far, you have studied the perfect cadence (V–I), the imperfect cadence (I–V, ii–V, IV–V, or vi–V), and the deceptive cadence (V–vi). A phrase may also end with a **plagal cadence** (IV–I). A plagal cadence often follows a perfect cadence.

The following progression contains a plagal cadence.

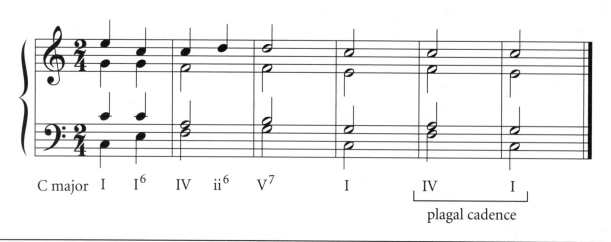

3. Add functional chord symbols and set the following figured basses containing plagal cadences.

(a)

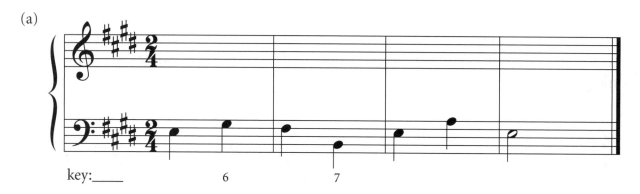

(b)

Lesson 20
Chord IV⁶ in Dominant Prolongation

IV^6 can be used as a passing chord between V_5^6 and V^7 or between V and V_5^6 to prolong dominant harmony. These prolongations lead to the tonic. V_5^6–I is a weaker perfect cadence than V^7–I because the dominant is not in the bass.

V_5^6–IV⁶–V⁷–I

In this progression, the third of IV^6 is doubled, which allows for voice exchange. Here, the voice exchange occurs between the bass and tenor (B–A–G and G–A–B). The common tone (F) is repeated, and V^7 resolves to I. Notice that the leading note descends in the progression V_5^6 to IV^6.

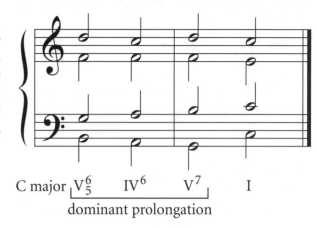

C major V_5^6 IV^6 V^7 I
dominant prolongation

C major   V   IV^6 V_5^6 I
dominant prolongation

V–IV⁶–V_5^6–I

The most common soprano line used with this progression consists of the scale degrees $\hat5$ $\hat4$ $\hat4$ $\hat3$. It is effective because the repeated scale degree $\hat4$ prepares the seventh of V_5^6. When IV^6 is used as a passing chord between V and V_5^6, the smoothest voice-leading is achieved by doubling the third of IV^6. Note the voice exchange in the example between the bass and alto (G–A–B and B–A–G). The leading note descends from V to IV^6. V_5^6 resolves in the usual manner to a complete chord I, with the leading note rising and the seventh falling.

When this progression is written in minor keys, the major IV chord with raised 6 must be used to avoid the melodic augmented 2nd between $\hat6$ and $\hat7$.

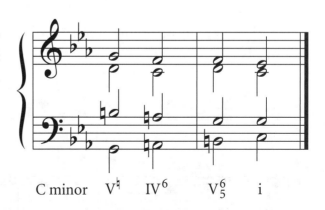

C minor   V♮   IV^6 V_5^6 i

CHORD IV⁶ IN DOMINANT PROLONGATION

1. Complete the following progressions for SATB.

2. Complete the following for four voices (SATB) according to the given chord symbols.

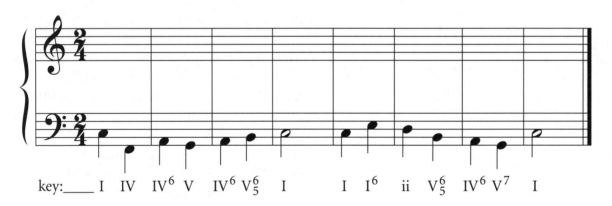

3. Provide a harmonic analysis of the following example using functional chord symbols.

LESSON 21
SECOND INVERSION ($^6_4$) CHORDS

Second-inversion chords are figured $^6_4$. These chords are not as stable as chords in root position or first inversion, and thus are not used as frequently. Second-inversion chords function as prolongations and decorations of other chords, and they are only used in certain progressions. *The bass note of the $^6_4$ chord is doubled.*

Cadential $^6_4$

Example ❷ below shows a prolongation of chord V by the $^6_4$ chord that precedes it. The $^6_4$ chord prolongs dominant harmony by delaying two notes of the dominant chord. The figures $^6_4$ and $^5_3$ refer to intervals above the bass note. Since this prolongation often happens at the cadence, it is called a **cadential $^6_4$**. The notes that make up the $^6_4$ are not part of the dominant chord and must resolve to the dominant chord tones which are a 5th and a 3rd above the bass. If you follow normal functional analysis, the $^6_4$ chord would be symbolized I^6_4, but in this progression the $^6_4$ chord does not have a tonic function. To show that the $^6_4$ is prolonging the dominant, it will be labeled V^{6-5}_{4-3}. Root/quality chord symbols also reflect this prolongation. In the example below, the cadential $^6_4$ is labeled $\frac{C}{G}\frac{G}{}$; this illustrates a C chord with a G in the bass, followed by a G chord with G in the bass. The line separating them confirms that it is really a prolongation of the dominant, G. The cadential $^6_4$ shown below is followed by I, creating a perfect cadence, but it may also be followed by vi, for a deceptive cadence (V^{6-5}_{4-3}–vi).

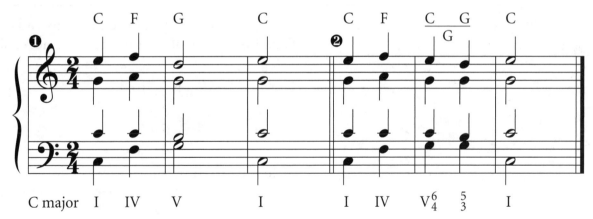

In the progression V^{6-5}_{4-3}, the bass remains on the dominant. The interval of a 6th falls to a 5th, the interval of a 4th falls to a 3rd, and the doubled bass note is repeated as a common tone. The notes of the $^6_4$ chord typically move down by step. *The cadential $^6_4$ usually occurs on a strong beat and its resolution on a weaker beat.* The bass may repeat, drop an octave, or be held. When writing the symbols for a cadential $^6_4$ in a minor key, the raised third is indicated with an accidental.

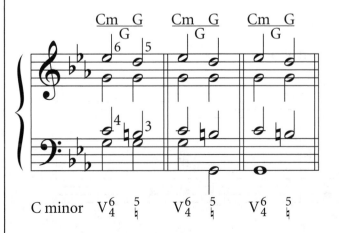

Second Inversion (⁶₄) Chords

1. Complete the following progressions for four voices.

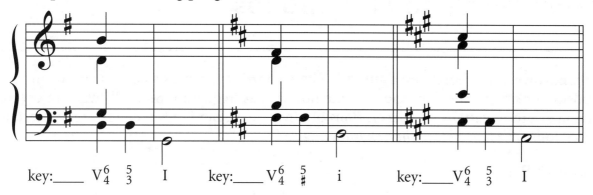

key:____ V⁶₄ ⁵₃ I   key:____ V⁶₄ ⁵♯ i   key:____ V⁶₄ ⁵₃ I

2. Write the following progressions for four voices.

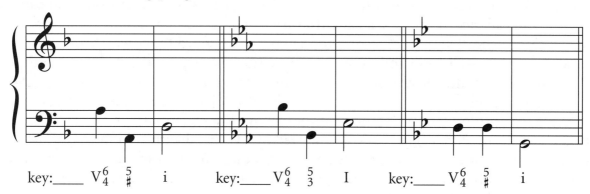

key:____ V⁶₄ ⁵♯ i   key:____ V⁶₄ ⁵₃ I   key:____ V⁶₄ ⁵♯ i

C major   ii   V⁸₆₄   ⁷₅₃   I

The cadential ⁶₄ may resolve to V⁷ instead of V. In this case, all of the three upper voices fall a step.

This progression is figured:

$$8 - 7$$
$$6 - 5$$
$$4 - 3$$

Note the rhythm in this example. The ⁶₄ usually occurs on a stronger beat than its resolution. This exception, in triple meter, may occur on beat 2.

3. Complete the following progressions for four voices.

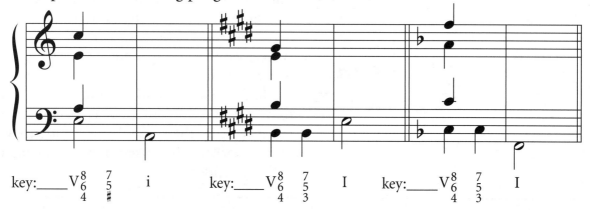

key:____ V⁸₆₄ ⁷₅♯ i   key:____ V⁸₆₄ ⁷₅₃ I   key:____ V⁸₆₄ ⁷₅₃ I

Approaching $^6_4$

Any chord that can precede V can precede a cadential $^6_4$. All pre-dominant chords, including IV, ii, and ii^6, are good choices. I and I^6 may also precede a cadential $^6_4$. The most active tone in the $^6_4$ chord is the 4th above the bass, which is also scale degree $\hat{1}$ of the key. If you use chord IV as a pre-dominant before a cadential $^6_4$, it is best to prepare the fourth with common-tone motion. If you use ii or ii^6, it is best to approach the fourth of $^6_4$ by step. This voice-leading is not absolutely necessary, but it is the most effective, and provides the smoothest motion to $^6_4$.

4. Provide a harmonic analysis of the following progressions using functional chord symbols. Study the movement from the pre-dominant to the $^6_4$ chords.

key:____

5. Complete the following progressions for four voices.

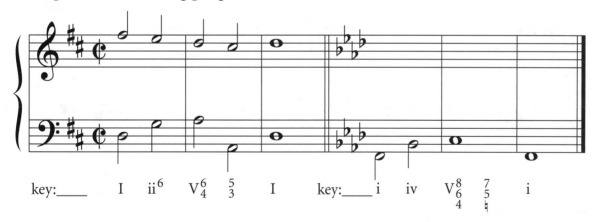

key:____   I   ii^6 V$^6_4$ $^5_3$ I   key:____ i   iv   V$^8_6$$_4$ $^7_5$ i

6. Set the following figured bass for four voices.

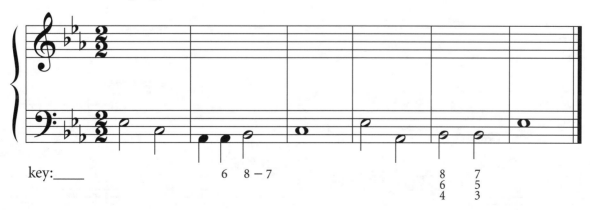

key:____   6   8 − 7   8   7
                                                  6   5
                                                  4   3

7. Name the key and provide a harmonic analysis of the following using functional chord symbols. Circle and identify any non-chord tones.

Sonata in C major
op. 20, no. 1 (2nd movement)

(a)

Friedrich Kuhlau
(1786–1832)

key:___

Sonatina in D major for Violin and Piano
op. posth. 137, no. 1, D 384 (2nd movement)

(b)

Franz Schubert
(1797–1828)

key:___

In instrumental writing, $^6_4$ chords may appear with different doubling and may resolve differently. There are basic principles with regard to doubling and resolution, but they are not absolute rules. Often the melody takes precedence over concerns about doubling, spacing, and resolution. Because of melodic considerations, the $^6_4$ chord in this example resolves in an irregular way. In order to produce more effective melodic lines, composers often ignore normal doubling and resolution conventions.

Songs without Words
op. 62, no. 28

Felix Mendelssohn
(1809–1847)

G major   V$^8_6$$_4$ $^7_5$$_3$ I

8. Name the key and provide a harmonic analysis of the following using both functional and root/quality chord symbols. Circle and identify any non-chord tones.

Sonatina in G minor for Violin and Piano
op. posth. 137, no. 3, D 408 (3rd movement)

(a)

Franz Schubert
(1797–1828)

key:____

Sonata in G minor for Violin and Piano
op. 137, no. 3, D 408

(b)

Franz Schubert
(1797–1828)

key:_____

Passing $^6_4$

The cadential $^6_4$ prolongs dominant harmony. The **passing** $^6_4$ prolongs tonic harmony.

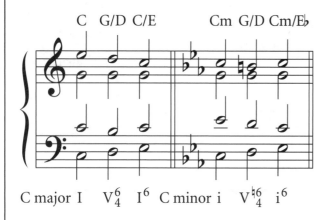

C major I V^6_4 I^6 C minor i $V^{\natural 6}_4$ i^6

V^6_4 can function as a passing chord between I and I^6 to prolong tonic harmony. Here, the V^6_4 is labeled as a second inversion dominant chord. This is different from the cadential $^6_4$ that prolongs dominant harmony. When a $^6_4$ chord prolongs tonic harmony, it is labeled in the same way that we have labeled all previous $^5_3$ and $^6_3$ chords. The root/quality chord symbol for this passing $^6_4$ is G/D, which indicates a G chord with a D as the lowest note. As usual, double the bass note of the $^6_4$ chord. In this progression, one voice keeps the common tone throughout, and one voice moves in neighbor motion. We call this chord a passing $^6_4$ because of the passing motion in the bass. Notice the two different soprano patterns: one uses voice exchange, and the other uses neighbor motion.

---

9.   Write the following passing $^6_4$ progressions.

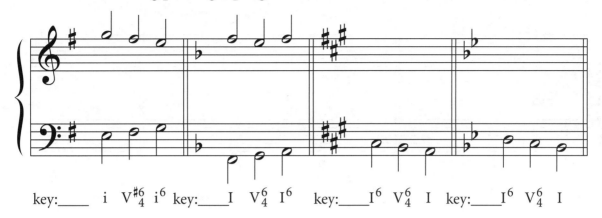

key:____ i V$^{\#6}_4$ i^6 key:____ I V$^6_4$ I^6 key:____ I^6 V$^6_4$ I   key:____ I^6 V$^6_4$ I

10.   Set the following figured bass for four voices.

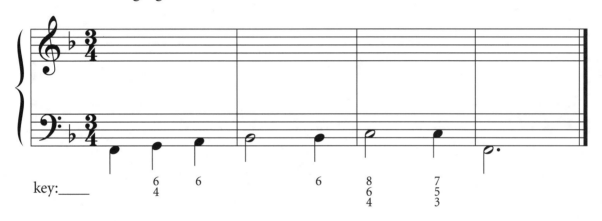

key:____   6   6   6   8   7
             4   6   5
                                    4   3

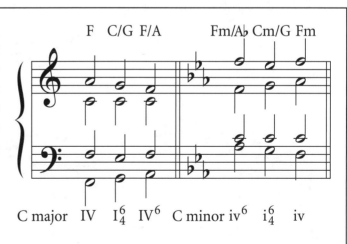

I$^6_4$ can function as a passing chord between IV and IV^6 to prolong the pre-dominant IV. In this progression, one voice keeps the common tone throughout, one voice moves in neighbor motion, and voice exchange occurs with one voice and the bass. In I$^6_4$, as in all $^6_4$ chords, the bass is normally doubled.

F C/G F/A   Fm/A♭ Cm/G Fm

C major   IV   I$^6_4$ IV^6 C minor   iv^6 i$^6_4$ iv

SECOND INVERSION ($^6_4$) CHORDS

11. Write the following passing $^6_4$ progressions.

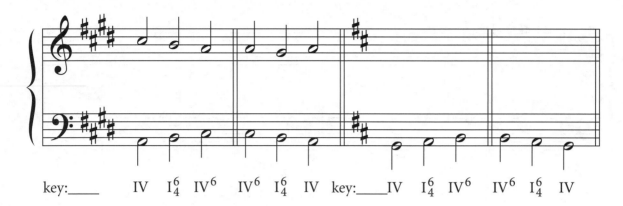

key:____ IV I$^6_4$ IV^6 IV^6 I$^6_4$ IV   key:____IV I$^6_4$ IV^6 IV^6 I$^6_4$ IV

12. Set the following figured bass for four voices.

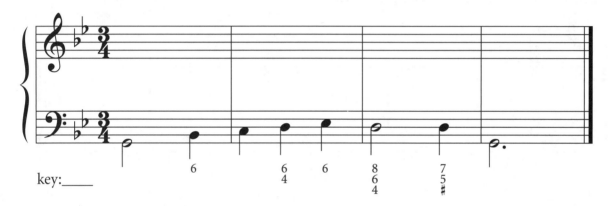

key:____

13. Provide a harmonic analysis of the following using functional chord symbols.

Piano Sonata
op. 2, no. 3

Ludwig van Beethoven
(1770–1827)

key:____

Neighboring $^6_4$

In the **neighboring** $^6_4$, the bass and one of the upper voices remain stationary while the two other voices move by step. Other names for this $^6_4$ progression are **stationary** or **pedal** $^6_4$, because of the stationary bass line.

I–IV$^6_4$–I and V–I$^6_4$–V

I–IV$^6_4$–I acts as a prolongation of tonic harmony. V–I$^6_4$–V acts as a prolongation of dominant harmony.

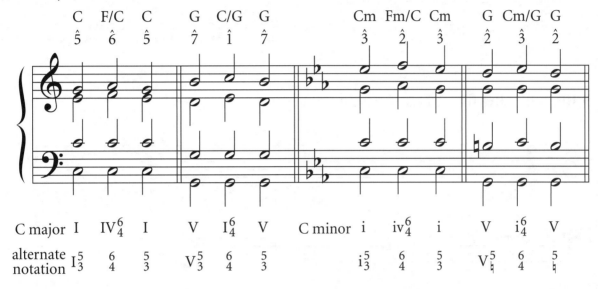

In each of the above progressions, the bass of the $^6_4$ chord is doubled and is repeated as a common tone. The two remaining voices move in neighbor motion above the stationary bass. The repeated octaves are not faulty parallels. Note the two different methods of symbolizing this progression. Both are correct.

IV$^6_4$ can be used to prolong an opening tonic, or to prolong a closing tonic after a perfect cadence.

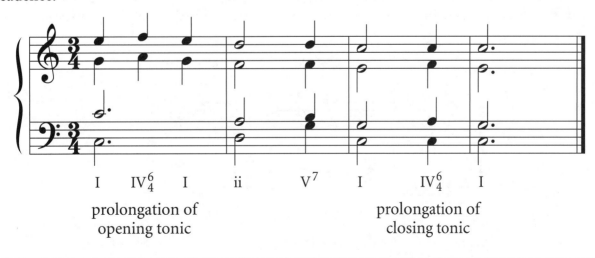

14. Write the following $\frac{6}{4}$ progressions.

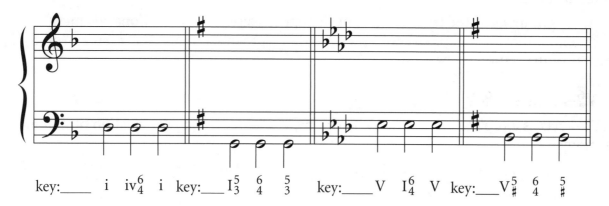

key:____ i iv$\frac{6}{4}$ i   key:____ I$\frac{5}{3}$ $\frac{6}{4}$ $\frac{5}{3}$ key:____ V I$\frac{6}{4}$ V   key:____ V$\frac{5}{\sharp}$ $\frac{6}{4}$ $\frac{5}{\sharp}$

15. Set the following figured bass for four voices.

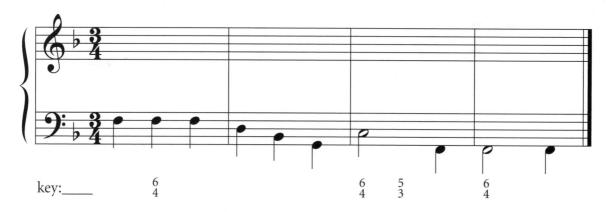

key:____ $\frac{6}{4}$ $\frac{6}{4}$ $\frac{5}{3}$ $\frac{6}{4}$

Arpeggio $\frac{6}{4}$

Like a first-inversion chord, a $\frac{6}{4}$ chord can be used to prolong a specific harmony. In each progression below, the bass outlines a chord. For example, the bass of I–I⁶–I$\frac{6}{4}$ is C E G, the I chord. Because a broken chord is called an arpeggio, the $\frac{6}{4}$ chords in these progressions are called **arpeggio $\frac{6}{4}$**.

C C/E C/G   F/A F/C F   G G/D G/B

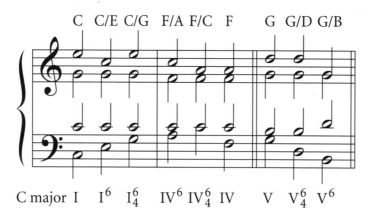

C major I   I⁶ I$\frac{6}{4}$ IV⁶ IV$\frac{6}{4}$ IV   V   V$\frac{6}{4}$ V⁶

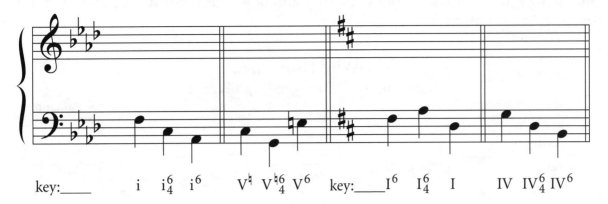

16. Complete the following progressions in four parts using arpeggio $^6_4$ progressions.

key:____   i   i$^6_4$ i^6 V$^\natural$ V$^{\natural 6}_4$ V^6 key:____I^6 I$^6_4$ I   IV IV$^6_4$ IV^6

17. Set the following figured basses with arpeggio $^6_4$ progressions.

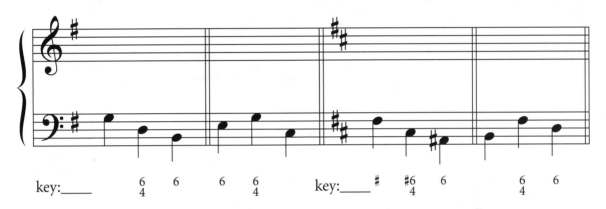

key:____ $^6_4$ 6   6 $^6_4$ key:____ #   #$^6_4$ 6 $^6_4$ 6

18. Provide a harmonic analysis of the following using both functional and root/quality chord symbols. Label the function of each $^6_4$ chord as cadential, neighboring, passing, or arpeggio.

key:____

19. Provide a harmonic analysis of the following using functional chord symbols. Circle and identify any non-chord tones. Identify and label the $^6_4$ chords and their functions (passing, cadential, etc.).

The Wild Horseman
from **Album für die Jugend, op. 68, no. 8**

(a)

Robert Schumann
(1810–1856)

key:____

Étude
op. 10, no. 5

(b)

Frédéric Chopin
(1810–1849)

key:____

Symphony no. 2 in D major
op. 36 (4th movement)

(c)

Ludwig van Beethoven
(1770–1827)

key:____

Piano Sonata in C major
K 309 (3rd movement)

(d)

Wolfgang Amadeus Mozart
(1756–1791)

key:____

Summary of Lesson 21

1. Second-inversion chords are symbolized as $^6_4$.

2. The bass note of a $^6_4$ chord is always doubled.

3. The cadential $^6_4$ prolongs the dominant at a cadence by delaying the notes of chord V in the upper voices.

4. The cadential $^6_4$ usually occurs on a beat that is stronger than its resolution. The exception to this is when it occurs on beat 2 in a triple meter.

5. The passing $^6_4$ prolongs tonic harmony in the progression I–V$^6_4$–I^6 or I^6–V$^6_4$–I. A passing $^6_4$ may also prolong the pre-dominant IV in the progressions IV–I$^6_4$–IV^6 and IV^6–I$^6_4$–IV.

6. In a neighboring $^6_4$, the bass remains stationary. Neighboring $^6_4$ progressions include I–IV$^6_4$–I and V–I$^6_4$–V.

7. An arpeggio $^6_4$ can be used to prolong a specific harmony. The bass moves in an arpeggio motion.

Lesson 22
Harmonic Rhythm

Harmonic rhythm refers to the number or pattern of harmonic changes in each measure of a piece of music. Music in a slower tempo generally has more harmonic changes than music in a faster tempo. The harmony usually changes on stronger beats, and over the bar line as the music moves from a weak to a strong beat. In the example below, the harmony changes on every quarter note until the cadence. Harmonic rhythm often changes at the cadence. Here, it changes to a half note for the final chord.

When analyzing harmonic rhythm, a prolongation of a chord using an inversion (for example, I–I⁶) is not considered a change of harmony.

Chorale no. 256: Jesu, deine tiefen Wunden
from **341 Four-Part Chorales**

Johann Sebastian Bach
(1685–1750)

The Schubert example below has a slow harmonic rhythm—the harmony changes only once per measure. When the harmonies change frequently, the harmonic rhythm is said to be fast.

When the harmonies change at a slower rate as in the example below, the harmonic rhythm is said to be slow.

Sonatina in G minor for Piano and Violin
op. posth. 137, no. 3, D 408

Franz Schubert
(1797–1828)

Here is a list of the common places for chord changes in three time signatures.

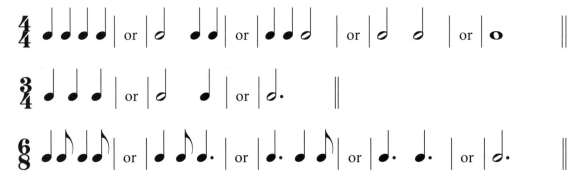

Chord changes should support the meter. Study the examples below.

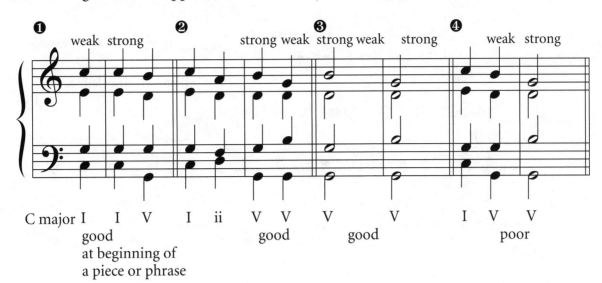

1. Repeating the tonic chord from a weak beat to a strong beat at the beginning of a composition or phrase is good because it emphasizes the tonality or key.

2. Repeating a chord from a strong to a weak beat is acceptable.

3. Repeating a chord from a strong beat through a weak beat to the next strong beat is acceptable.

4. Avoid repeating a chord from a weak to a strong beat. The ear expects something strong when music moves from a weak to a strong beat. If the chord remains the same, it sounds as if the strong beat has not arrived, and gives the illusion that the time signature has changed.

1. Provide a harmonic analysis using functional chord symbols and state the harmonic rhythm under each example.

Chorus: "Das klinget…"
from *The Magic Flute,* act 1, scene 3, K 620

(a)

Wolfgang Amadeus Mozart
(1756–1791)

key: ____

harmonic analysis:

harmonic rhythm:

Chorale no. 125: Allein Gott in der Höh' sei Ehr'
from 371 Four-Part Chorales

(b)

Johann Sebastian Bach
(1685–1750)

key:____

harmonic analysis:

harmonic rhythm:

Nocturne in G minor
op. 37, no. 1

(c)

Frédéric Chopin
(1810–1849)

Andante sostenuto

key:____

harmonic analysis:

harmonic rhythm:

Toccata in D minor
L 422/K 141

(d)

Domenico Scarlatti
(1685–1757)

key:_____

harmonic analysis:

harmonic rhythm:

Lesson 23
Melody Writing 1

In this lesson, you will learn to write a one-phrase answer to a given melody, using a type of melody writing called **question and answer** or **antecedent and consequent**.

Here are some general rules to follow:

1. The first phrase ends with an open cadence, and the second with a closed cadence.

2. If the first phrase begins with an upbeat, the responding phrase will also begin with an upbeat.

3. The final melody notes of the responding phrase will be leading note to tonic ($\hat{7}$–$\hat{1}$) or supertonic to tonic ($\hat{2}$–$\hat{1}$).

Here is the opening phrase of a famous melody by Beethoven. Notice that the phrase ends on an imperfect cadence (I–V).

Symphony no. 9 in D minor
(4th movement)

Ludwig van Beethoven
(1770–1827)

One of the easiest ways to write a response to this four-measure phrase is to repeat the phrase, but change the ending so that it fits a perfect cadence. This can be done by changing the final melody notes to the leading note and tonic ($\hat{7}$–$\hat{1}$) or the supertonic and tonic ($\hat{2}$–$\hat{1}$).

Here, Beethoven chose supertonic–to–tonic, which supports a perfect cadence and gives a satisfying answer to the first phrase.

MELODY WRITING 1

1. For each example, name the key, mark the phrases, and add a tempo marking. Write a responding phrase to answer the given openings to create a unified melodic composition. Add full functional chord symbols and a bass part at the cadences. Add rests in the bass to complete each measure.

(a)   Tempo:_____

key:___

Hint: Start the responding phrase with an upbeat.

(b)   Tempo:_____

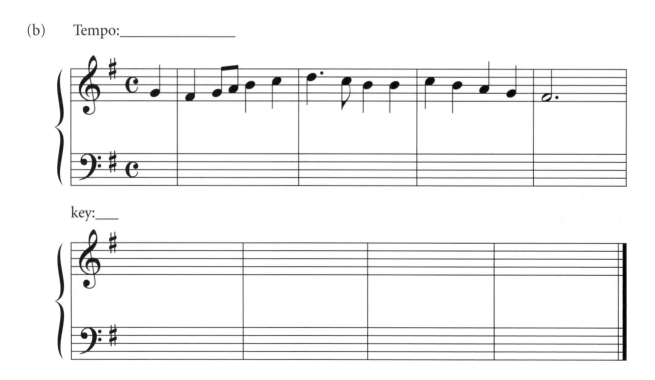

key:___

Minor Key Melodies

When writing melodies, it is important to avoid dissonant melodic intervals such as augmented 2nds or augmented 4ths, since they usually create an unmusical melodic line. When writing a response to a melody in a minor key, it is advisable to use the ascending or descending form of the melodic minor scale. This will prevent the awkward augmented 2nd that occurs between $\hat{6}$ and raised $\hat{7}$.

G harmonic minor

G melodic minor

G minor

Avoid melodic augmented 4ths.

G minor

Diminished 5ths may be used as long as they are resolved by a note within the compass of the interval.

The melody below is in the key of G minor. By using the melodic form of the minor scale, raising $\hat{6}$ and $\hat{7}$, a dissonant augmented 2nd is avoided in the response.

MELODY WRITING 1

1. For each example, name the key, mark the phrases, and add a tempo marking. Write responding phrases to create a unified melodic composition. Add full functional chord symbols and a bass part at the cadences. Add rests in the bass to complete each measure.

(a)   Tempo:_____

key:_____

Hint: Start the responding phrase with an upbeat.

(b)   Tempo:_____

key:_____

Implied Harmony

A melody suggests a particular harmony. This harmony is called the **implied harmony**.

Example ❶ implies the tonic chord (I) because it outlines the notes of that chord (C E G).

Example ❷ implies the dominant chord (V) because it outlines G B D.

Example ❸ implies two harmonies: ii (D F A) or IV (F A C). If a chord implies two harmonies, choose the one that makes the most musical and harmonic sense in the progression.

Example ❹ implies the same two harmonies (ii or IV) but it contains a non-chord tone (passing tone).

Example ❺ has a repeated note that can imply I, IV, or vi, because C is contained in all three chords. The choice of chord here may depend on the chords that precede and follow, bearing in mind the progression at hand. A single repeated note can imply one harmony or two different harmonies, depending on the progression.

Even the very simplest melodies can imply more than one harmony. Choosing chords to harmonize a melody is not always a question of being right or wrong. Instead, it is a matter of choosing an appropriate chord progression that fits with the style and structure of the melody. Sing and play the melody, and let your ear and your knowledge of harmony decide which chords are best suited for the harmony.

Steps for Choosing Harmony for a Given Melody

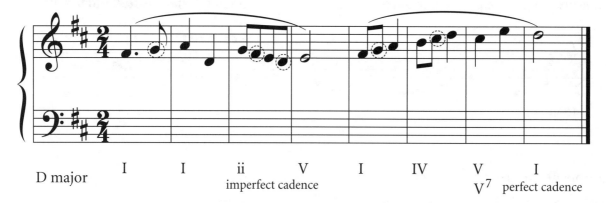

D major   I   I   ii   V   I   IV   V   I

                                  imperfect cadence V^7 perfect cadence

1. Find the phrase endings and choose the cadences. The most likely choices are perfect and imperfect.
2. Choose the pre-cadential chords. A different chord than the two cadence chords is best, but an inversion of one of these chords may also be used.
3. Choose the chords for the remainder of the melody. Remember that primary chords, especially at the beginning, will help to establish the key of the melody.
4. Be aware of the non-chord tones. Do not let them confuse your choice of harmony. The circled notes in the above example are non-chord tones.
5. Chord symbols used for this type of exercise to show the implied harmony indicate only harmonic functions. Except at cadences where a bass line is written, they do not indicate chord positions.

1. Name the key and add phrasing and functional chord symbols to the following melodies to indicate the implied harmony.

(a)

key:_____

implied harmony:

(b)

key:_____

implied harmony:

Rhythm at Cadence Points

As a general rule, the second chord of a cadence should not fall on a weak beat. The example below is poor because the dominant chord of the imperfect cadence falls on a weaker beat than the tonic chord that precedes it. It is also weak because it does not follow the implied harmony. The end of m. 3 implies ii or IV, and we expect V to follow.

Here is a better solution for a cadence at the end of this phrase. The phrase still ends with an imperfect cadence, but the dominant chord is placed on a stronger beat than chord ii that precedes it.

There are, however, exceptions to the above rule. In $\frac{6}{8}$ time, a cadence ending on beat 2 (pulse 4) can be quite effective.

A melodic sequence can be used as a responsive phrase to a given melody. This is achieved by repeating the given phrase at a higher or lower interval. It is important to be aware of the harmony that the melody implies. In the example below, the first phrase ends on the scale degree $\hat{2}$. If you write the response a 2nd lower, it will end on $\hat{1}$ with a perfect cadence. Occasionally, a slight variation at the end of the phrase may be needed in order to end with a perfect cadence. This technique may not be effective if the melody outlines a series of chords. The final melody notes should be $\hat{7}-\hat{1}$ or $\hat{2}-\hat{1}$. If a sequential repetition results in weak harmony, you can either not use the sequence, or else vary it to improve the harmonic implications.

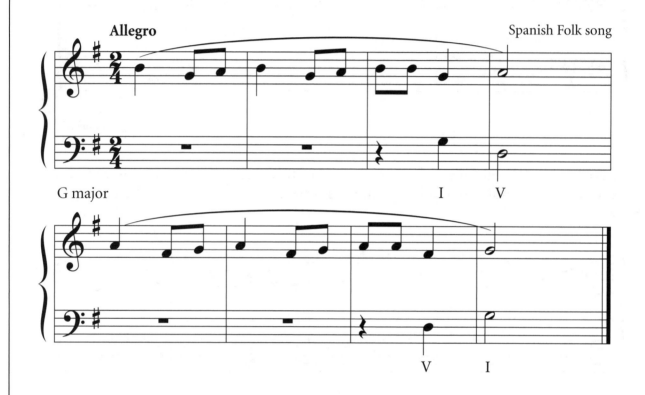

Be careful when writing a response up or down a 2nd. If the melody contains the interval of a perfect 4th, you may end up with an augmented 4th in the resulting response. For now, you should avoid augmented intervals between melody notes.

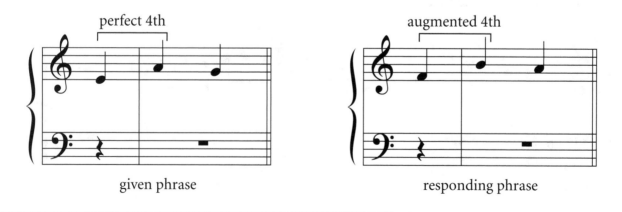

given phrase   responding phrase

Another option for writing a responding phrase is to repeat it sequentially down a 4th or up a 5th. This moves the phrase into the dominant. Be aware of the harmony that the melody implies. The responding melody in the example below was created by writing the original phrase down a 4th and varying the ending. The responding phrase ends $\hat{7}$–$\hat{1}$, supporting a perfect cadence. Sometimes an exact sequential repetition is not possible and some adjustment of the melody will be required.

1. For each example, mark the phrases and add a tempo marking. Add both functional and root/quality chord symbols indicating the implied harmony throughout. Write responding phrases to answer the given openings, creating a unified melodic composition.

(a) Tempo:_____

key:_____

MELODY WRITING 1

Piano Sonata in C major
Hob. XVI:35 (1st movement)

(b)   Tempo:_____

Franz Joseph Haydn
(1732–1809)

key:_____

Implied Harmony

The following melodic fragments occurring at the end of a phrase can imply a $^6_4$ decoration of chord V. Remember that a cadential $^6_4$ occurs on a strong beat in the measure, or on a strong part of the beat. At the end of a phrase, an imperfect cadence (I–V) on these two notes would be less effective, since the second chord of the cadence should fall on a stronger beat than the first. If these examples were found in the middle of a phrase, they could imply two different chords.

The following melody ends in a cadential $^6_4$.

Piano Sonata in A major
K 331

Wolfgang Amadeus Mozart
(1756–1791)

1. Name the key, and add phrasing and functional chord symbols to the following melody to indicate the implied harmony.

key:_____

implied harmony:

Another technique for a melodic response is to write a variation of the melody and rhythm of the original phrase, ending with scale degrees $\hat{7}$–$\hat{1}$ or $\hat{2}$–$\hat{1}$.

In the example below, melodic and rhythmic variation is achieved by the addition of passing tones. The first phrase ends in an imperfect cadence with the V chord decorated by $^6_4$. The final melody notes are scale degrees $\hat{3}$–$\hat{2}$–$\hat{1}$, supporting a perfect cadence decorated by a cadential $^6_4$. The chord symbols indicating the harmony implied by the melody are included.

1. For each example, name the key, mark the phrasing, and add an appropriate tempo. Add functional chord symbols indicating the implied harmony throughout. Write a responding phrase to the given opening, creating a unified melodic composition. Use various melodic techniques studied up to this point.

(a)

key:____

(b)

key:____

LESSON 24
THE SUPERTONIC 7TH CHORD

The supertonic 7th (ii[7]) chord is built on the second degree of the scale, by adding a seventh to the ii chord.

In major keys, ii[7] is a minor 7th chord consisting of a minor triad and a minor 7th.

In minor keys, ii[7] is a half-diminished 7th chord consisting of a diminished triad and a minor 7th. A fully diminished 7th chord is a diminished triad with a diminished 7th above the root.

The half-diminished 7th chord is symbolized by a small circle with a line through it (ø).

The root position of the supertonic 7th (ii[7]) functions as a pre-cadential chord before V or V[7]. You must prepare the seventh of ii[7] by repeating it as a common tone from the previous chord. It resolves downward by step to the third of chord V. You may either use the complete chord or omit the fifth and double the root or third of ii[7] in root position. However, the chord should be complete when it is used in inversion.

In Example ❶ below, the seventh of ii[7] (C) is prepared in the soprano, and the root of ii[7] is doubled. This doubling helps to avoid faulty parallel 5ths between the tenor and bass. The seventh of ii[7] resolves downward by step to the third of V[7].

In minor keys, faulty parallel 5ths are not a problem between i and ii[ø7]. The 5ths in Example ❷, between the tenor and bass in the progression i–ii[ø7], are not incorrect because one is a perfect 5th and one is a diminished 5th.

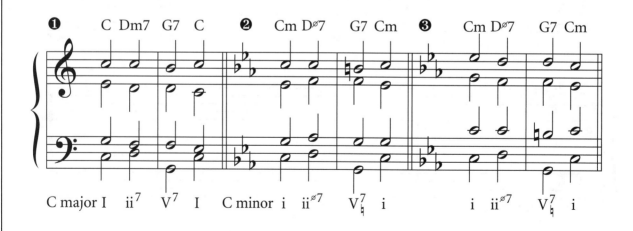

1. Complete the following progressions for four voices. Prepare and resolve the sevenths in ii⁷.

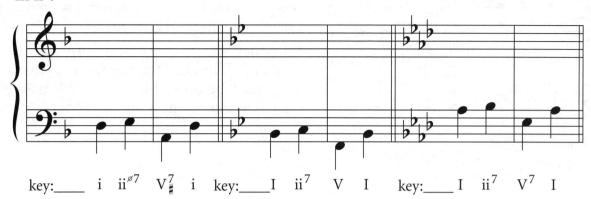

key:____ i ii°⁷ V⁷♯ i   key:____ I ii⁷ V I   key:____ I ii⁷ V⁷ I

Inversions of ii⁷

Inversions of ii⁷ are symbolized ii$^6_5$, ii$^4_3$, and ii$^4_2$ (similar to inversions of V⁷). All supertonic 7th chords function as pre-dominant chords. The ii$^6_5$ chord is used more often than the other inversions—ii$^6_5$ usually leads to V or V$^{8\text{-}7}$. Since scale degree $\hat{4}$ is in the bass of ii$^6_5$, it usually moves to 5.

A ii$^6_5$ can also lead to a cadential $^6_4$. In this progression, the resolution is delayed. The seventh must stay in the same voice, then resolve downward as usual.

In the following ii$^6_5$–V progressions, the seventh resolves down by step, and the common tone is repeated in the same voice. Note the soprano patterns.

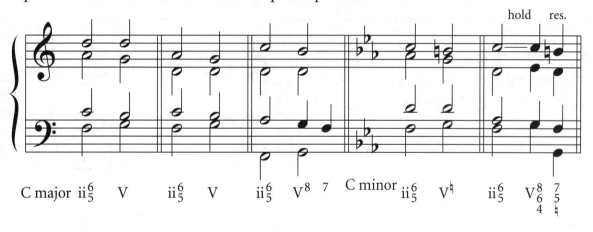

C major ii$^6_5$ V   ii$^6_5$ V   ii$^6_5$ V$^{8\ 7}$ C minor ii$^6_5$ V$^♮$ ii$^6_5$ V$^{8\ 7}_{6\ 5}_{4\ ♮}$

---

2. Complete the following progressions.

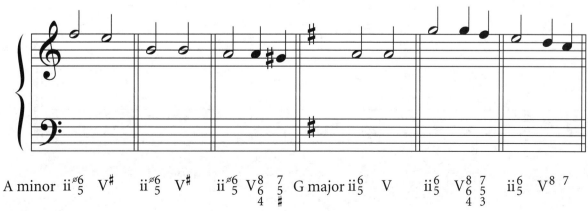

A minor ii°$^6_5$ V♯   ii°$^6_5$ V♯   ii°$^6_5$ V$^{8\ 7}_{6\ 4\ ♯}$ G major ii$^6_5$ V   ii$^6_5$ V$^{8\ 7}_{6\ 5\ 4\ 3}$ ii$^6_5$ V$^{8\ 7}$

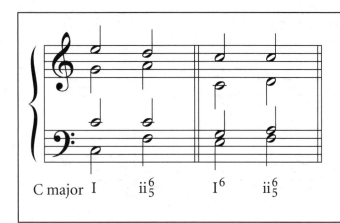

When joining I to ii$^6_5$, the seventh is prepared and all other motion is stepwise.

A ii$^6_5$ may also follow a tonic prolongation. When ii$^6_5$ follows I^6, the seventh is prepared. Care must be taken to avoid faulty parallel motion in this progression.

3. Set the following figured bass for four voices.

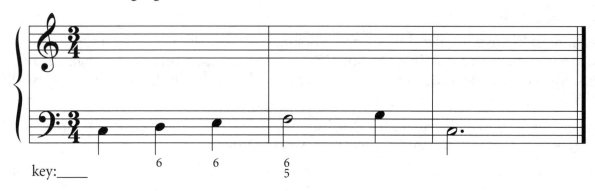

A ii$^6_5$ can occur in tonic prolongation before V$^4_2$. The seventh in each chord is prepared and resolved by step downwards.

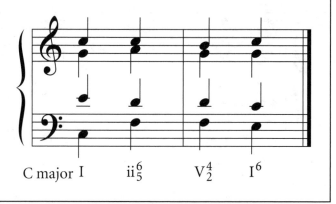

4. Complete the following progression for four voices.

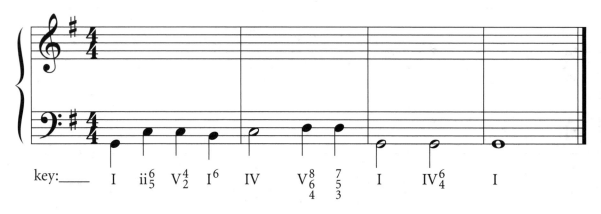

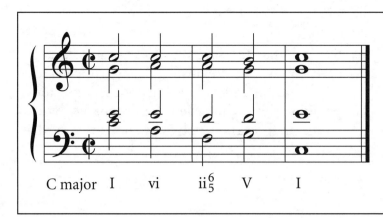

C major   I   vi   ii$_5^6$ V   I

A ii$_5^6$ may follow vi in a descending-3rd progression. The seventh of ii$_5^6$ is prepared by common-tone motion. Here, vi acts as a link between the opening tonic (I) and the pre-dominant (ii$_5^6$).

5.   Complete the following progression for four voices.

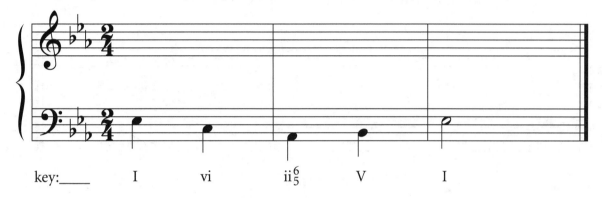

key:____   I   vi   ii$_5^6$ V   I

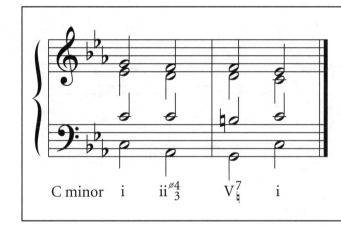

C minor   i   ii$_3^{ø4}$ V$_\sharp^7$ i

A ii$_3^4$ can be used as a pre-dominant before V or V^7. The sevenths are prepared and resolve by step downward.

6.   Complete the following progressions for four voices.

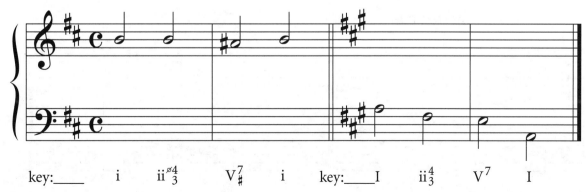

key:____   i   ii$_3^{ø4}$ V$_\sharp^7$ i   key:____ I   ii$_3^4$ V^7 I

THE SUPERTONIC 7TH CHORD

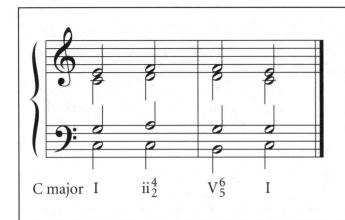

Since ii_2^4 has the seventh in the bass, and the seventh resolves downward by step, it leads to V_5^6 or occasionally V^6. The ii_2^4 is used in tonic prolongation. The seventh is prepared by a common tone and resolves by step downward.

C major   I ii_2^4 V_5^6 I

7.   Complete the following progressions for four voices.

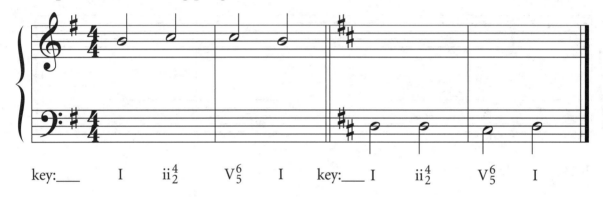

key:___   I ii_2^4 V_5^6 I   key:___   I ii_2^4 V_5^6 I

I^6 may act as a passing chord between the root position and the first inversion of the supertonic 7th (in either order). This is a prolongation of the supertonic 7th. Here, it occurs between ii^7 and ii_5^6. Note the doubled third in I^6.

The seventh of ii^7 is repeated as a common tone in all three chords, and then resolves downward to the third of V or V^7.

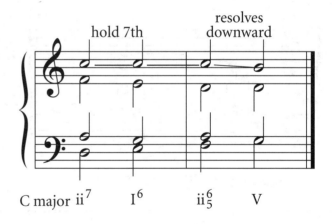

hold 7th   resolves downward

C major ii^7 I^6 ii_5^6 V

8.   Set the following figured bass for four voices.

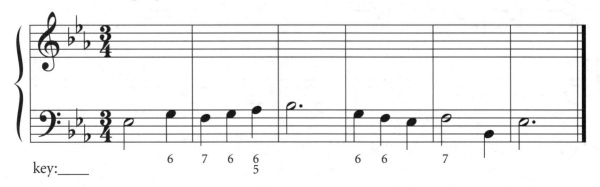

key:___   6   7   6   6   6   6   7
                                            5

Often there may be more than one way to analyze a musical excerpt. The following example shows two different but equally correct analyses of the same passage. If both functional and root/quality symbols are used, they must be consistent. If, as in example ❶, you choose to label the second chord Dm7/F, it must also be labeled as ii$_5^6$. If you choose to label it as Fmaj7 as in example ❷, the functional chord symbols must be IV7. The non-chord tones must also reflect the analyzed harmony. Study these examples and notice how the function of the non-chord tones changes with the choice of harmony.

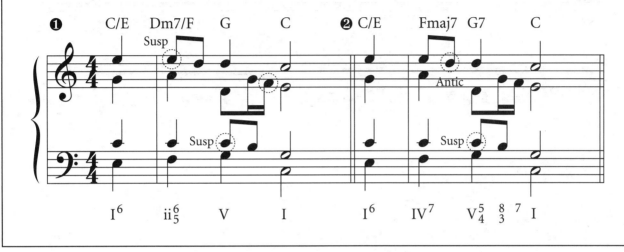

9. Provide a harmonic analysis of the following excerpt using both functional and root/quality chord symbols.

A Chorale
from **Album für die Jugend, op. 68, no. 4**

Robert Schumann
(1810–1856)

10. Provide a harmonic analysis of the following using functional and root/quality chord symbols. Label any non-chord tones.

Serenade
No. 4 from *Schwanengesang*

(a)

key:_____

Lei - se fle - hen mei - ne Lie - der durch die Nacht‿zu dir.

Nocturne in C minor
op. 48, no. 1

(b)

Frédéric Chopin
(1810–1849)

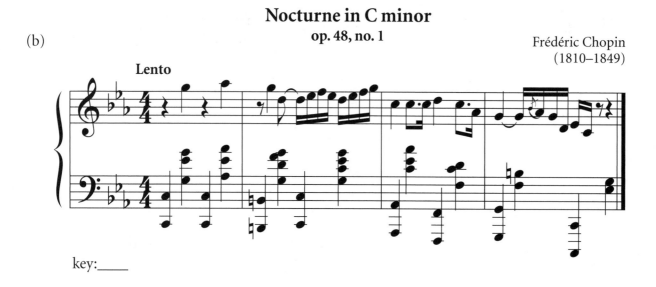

key:____

Symphony no. 5 in E minor
op. 64 (2nd movement)

Pyotr Il'yich Tchaikovsky
(1840–1893)

(c)

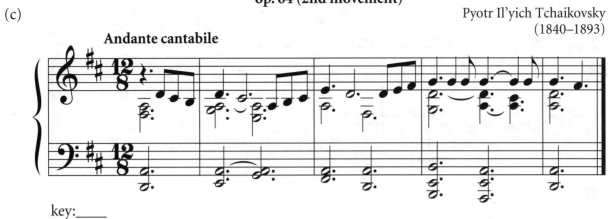

key:____

11. Complete the following examples for four voices according to the given chord symbols.

(a)

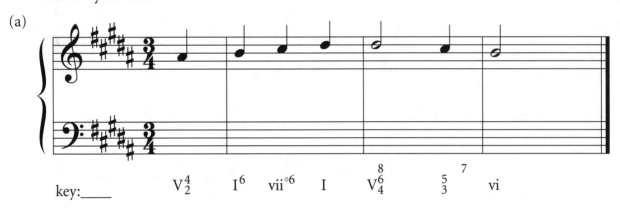

key:____ V_2^4 I^6 vii$^{\circ 6}$ I V_4^6 $^8_{~}$ $^{~5}_{~3}$ ^{7} vi

(b)

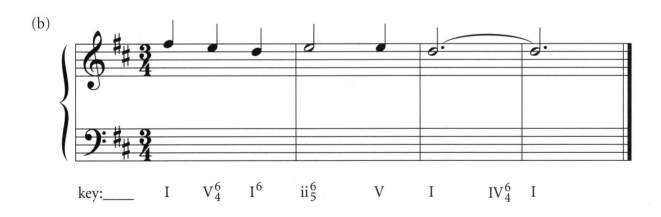

key:____ I V_4^6 I^6 ii$_5^6$ V I IV_4^6 I

The Supertonic 7th Chord

12. Set the following figured basses for four voices.

(a)

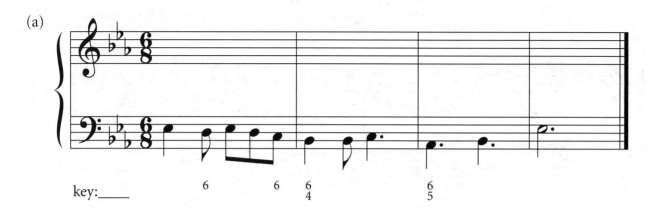

key:____

(b)

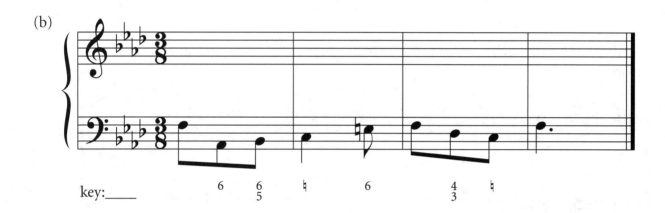

key:____

13. Complete the following melody for SATB.

key:____

SUMMARY OF LESSON 24

1. The ii^7 chord and its inversions are pre-dominant chords.

2. The seventh of ii^7 is prepared by a common tone and resolves downward by step to the dominant harmony. A cadential $^6_4$ decorating V delays the resolution of the seventh of ii^7.

3. The ii^7 chord is most often used in the progression I–ii^7–V$^{(7)}$–I.

4. In minor keys, the ii^7 chord is often written as an incomplete chord with the fifth omitted and the root doubled. This helps to avoid faulty parallels.

5. All inversions of ii^7 (ii$^6_5$, ii$^4_3$, and ii$^4_2$) are written as complete chords containing root, third, fifth, and seventh.

6. I^6 may act as a passing chord between ii^7 and ii$^6_5$, or between ii$^6_5$ and ii^7, prolonging supertonic harmony.

LESSON 25
APPLIED DOMINANTS

The movement of music from one key to another is called modulation or tonicization. Modulation implies a relatively long change of key while tonicization is a short shift. The tonicization of chord V means that V becomes a temporary tonic and is preceded by its own dominant. Major keys move to the dominant more often than any other key, because V is the most important chord after I. When a chord becomes the dominant of another key it is called an **applied** or **secondary dominant**.

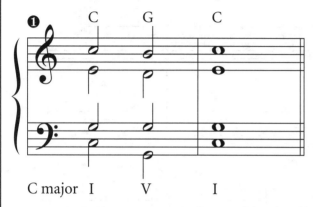

C major   I   V   I

The progression in Example ❶ does not tonicize the dominant.

In the progression in Example ❷, V is tonicized (made a temporary tonic). The dominant of V is placed in front of it. An accidental is needed because V in G major is D F♯ A (G major has an F sharp). It may be necessary to cancel this accidental if F natural is used later in the same measure. All V/V chords have an accidental on the third. V/V is resolved in the same way that V is resolved to I. The oral expression of V/V is "five of five."

C major   I   V/V   V^{8} ^{7} I

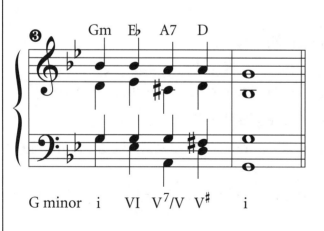

G minor   i   VI   V^{7}/V   V$^{\sharp}$ i

In Example ❸, V^{7}/V precedes V. The third of V^{7} is raised to accommodate the new key of D major (which has a C♯ in its key signature). V^{7}/V resolves to V in the same way that V^{7} resolves to I. The oral expression of V^{7}/V is "five-seven of five."

In these examples, the accidental in V^{7}/V is not shown in the chord symbols. Applied dominants are assumed to have major 3rds. This applies to the secondary dominant when the Roman numeral is present. In a figured bass, when no Roman numerals are present, the accidentals must be shown in the figuration. Since root/quality chord symbols do not address the function of the chord, V7/V is symbolized for what it is: here, a major-minor 7th, or dominant 7th on A (A7).

1. Analyze the following progressions by providing functional chord symbols.

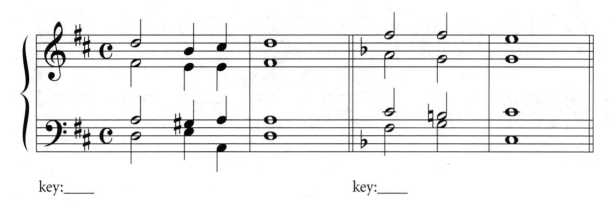

key:____   key:____

V/V or V⁷/V may be used in inversion. All inversions of V⁷/V are effective.
Study the examples below.

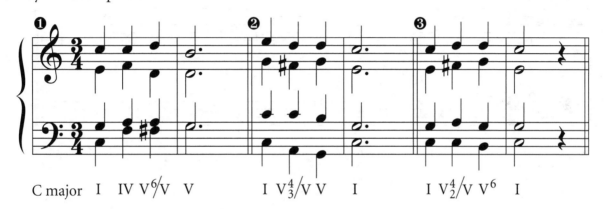

C major   I   IV   V^6/V   V   I   V$^4_3$/V   V   I   I   V$^4_2$/V   V^6 I

In Example ❶, the chromatic semitone F–F♯ is kept in the same voice.

Example ❷ contains the second inversion of V⁷/V.

In Example ❸, V$^4_2$/V resolves to V^6 since the seventh is in the bass and must fall. Notice that the seventh of V⁷/V is prepared by common-tone motion and resolves downward by step.

---

2. Complete the following progressions for four voices.

(a)

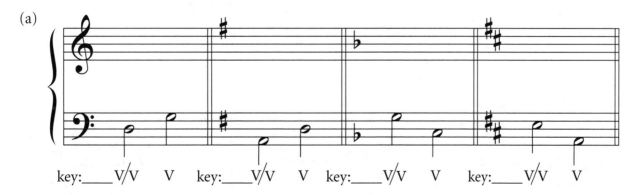

key:____ V/V   V   key:____ V/V   V   key:____ V/V   V   key:____ V/V   V

(b)

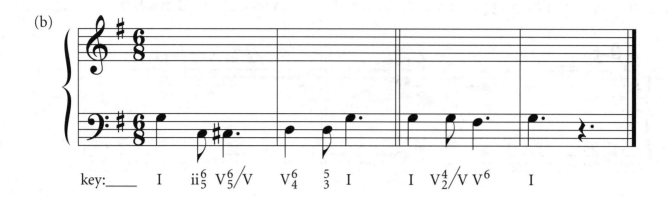

key:____ I ii$_5^6$ V$_5^6$/V V$_4^6$ $_3^5$ I I V$_2^4$/V V^6 I

3. Complete the following example by adding functional chord symbols, and alto and tenor voices.

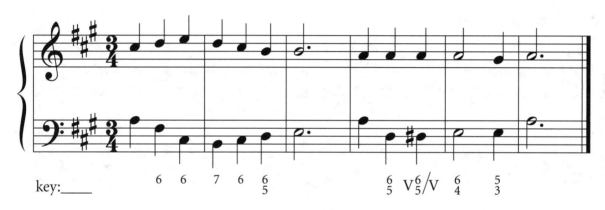

key:____ 6 6 7 6 6$_5$ 6$_5$ V$_5^6$/V 6$_4$ 5$_3$

4. Set the following figured bass for four voices.

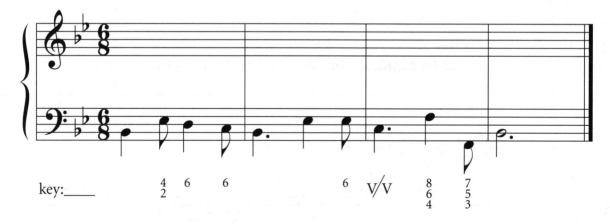

key:____ 4$_2$ 6 6 6 V/V 8$_6$$_4$ 7$_5$$_3$

5. Name the key, symbolize the chords with functional and root/quality chord symbols, and circle and identify any non-chord tones.

Sonatina
op. 57, no. 1 (2nd movement)

Albert Biehl
(1835–1899)

key:____

6. For the following excerpts, name the key, symbolize the chords with functional and root/quality chord symbols, and circle and classify any non-chord tones.

Chorale no. 106: Jesu Leiden, Pein und Tod
from 371 Four-Part Chorales

(a)

Johann Sebastian Bach
(1685–1750)

Sonatina in G major
no. 2 of 12 Sonatines progressives (2nd movement)

Johann Baptist Vaňhal
(1739–1813)

(b)

key:____

Sonatina
op. 20, no. 1

(c)

Fritz Spindler
(1817–1905)

key:____

Chorus: The Heavens Are Telling
no. 14 from The Creation, Hob. XXI: 2

(d)

Franz Joseph Haydn
(1732–1809)

key:___

Chorale no. 288: Gelobet seist du, Jesu Christ
from 371 Four-Part Chorales

Johann Sebastian Bach
(1685–1750)

(e)

key:___

7. Complete the following progressions for four voices (SATB) according to the given chord symbols.

(a)

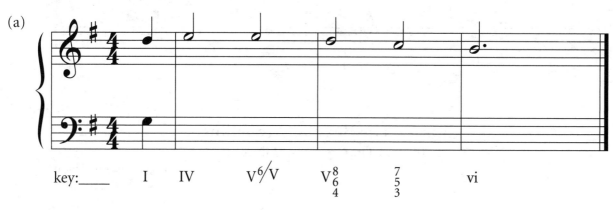

key:___   I   IV   V⁶/V   V$^8_{6}_{4}$ $^7_5_3$ vi

(b)

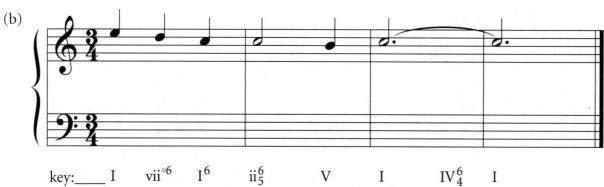

key:___   I   vii°⁶   I⁶   ii$^6_5$ V   I   IV$^6_4$ I

(c)

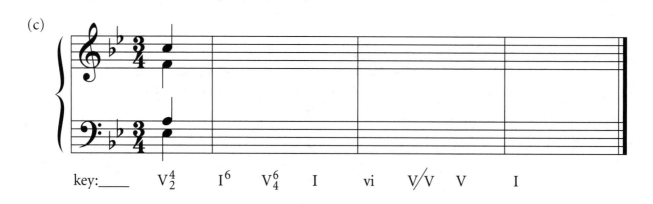

key:___   V$^4_2$ I⁶   V$^6_4$ I   vi   V/V   V   I

8. Complete the following excerpt for four voices (SATB). Show all functional chord symbols.

Chorale no. 42: Du Friedensfürst, Herr Jesu Christ
from **371 Four-Part Chorales**

Johann Sebastian Bach
(1685–1750)

---

vii°⁶/V

You will learn about two types of applied chords. $V^{(7)}$ bears a dominant relationship to the chord that follows it. The other applied chord is vii, which bears a leading-note relationship to the chord that follows. Both of these chords have the same harmonic function. The leading note is a strong tendency tone and resolves to the tonic.

In the example below, V is tonicized by placing its leading-note triad in front of it. Here, the strong pull from F sharp to G identifies G as the temporary tonic. The vii chord is a diminished triad in this progression, and is used in first inversion. *Remember that the temporary leading note in vii⁶ is not doubled.*

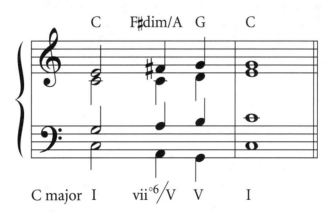

APPLIED DOMINANTS

1. Write the following progressions in four-part (SATB) style. These examples are in major keys.

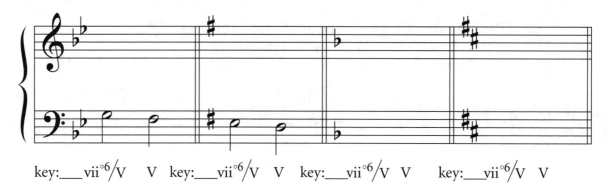

key:___vii°⁶/V V   key:___vii°⁶/V V   key:___vii°⁶/V V   key:___vii°⁶/V V

2. Write the following progressions in four-part (SATB) style.

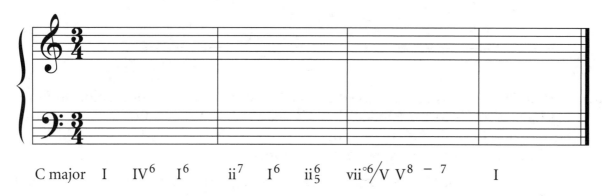

C major   I   IV⁶   I⁶   ii⁷   I⁶   ii⁶₅   vii°⁶/V V⁸ ⁻ ⁷   I

LESSON 26
MODULATION

Secondary dominants or tonicizations are short gestures into a new key area. They do not last long enough for the ear to recognize them as new tonal centers. **Modulation** occurs when the tonicization lasts longer, with several chords that function in the new key, creating a new tonal center.

Unless it is very short, a piece written in a single key can lack interest. Changing key by modulating can add interest, tonal variety, and contribute to the form of a piece of music.

In modulation, the new key usually contains one or more notes that are not part of the original key. These notes help to direct the ear to the new tonal center. The exception to this is when you modulate from a minor key to its relative major since both use the same key signature.

Study the following excerpt, which includes a modulation from the key of C major to the key of G major. One of the new accidentals that occurs during a modulation is often, but not always, the leading note of the new key. This is because the dominant of the new key is used to modulate and the leading note is part of the dominant. Occasionally, notes that are foreign to the key appear in a passage, but these are not always an indication of a modulation. In m. 4, the F♯ is a chromatic lower neighbour and not a reflection of a key change. Plus, the music returns to F natural within the same measure. The new key is signaled by the prominence of notes or chords that have structural importance in that key. They are either repeated or they form part of a cadence. The shift to G major begins in m. 8 with the scale passage containing F♯. This F♯ remains throughout the rest of the example and the key is firmly established with the repeated appearance of V^7 and I in G major.

For the following excerpt: name the key and provide a harmonic analysis using both functional and root/quality chord symbols. Circle and classify any non-chord tones.

Sonatina
op. 55, no. 1 (1st movement)

Friedrich Kuhlau
(1786–1832)

key:____

From the preceding example we can see that the modulation is established through the dominant and tonic chords in the new key of G major. This is reinforced with the repetition of chords in G major and perfect cadences in G major. Cadences aid in clearly establishing a tonal center.

Modulations from a minor key to its relative major are not as clear since there may be no accidentals indicating the new key. The following piece begins in D minor and modulates to F major. The first measure is made up of tonic and dominant harmony in D minor. The second measure begins the modulation to F major and the rest of the phrase consists mainly of tonic and dominant harmony in F major.

In this example, no accidentals are required to modulate. Here, it is actually the absence of an accidental (C♯) that indicates a key other than D minor. It is important to note that the majority of modulations will contain accidentals indicating the new key, but this is not always the case. In this example, no accidentals are needed to modulate to the relative major. We must look at the chord progressions to determine what is happening harmonically. As in the previous example, dominant harmony is used prominently and frequently to take us to the new key.

Jigg
from **Suite in D minor, HWV 437**

George Frideric Handel
(1685–1759)

Modulation to Closely Related Keys

Key relationships are important in modulation. A composition may modulate to a **closely related key.** Two keys are closely related if their key signatures have a difference of no more than one sharp or one flat. D major (two sharps) and A major (three sharps) are closely related because there is a difference of only one sharp.

There are five closely related keys to any major or minor key:

• The relative major or minor of the original key.

• The pair of relative major and minor keys with one more sharp or flat than the original key.

• The pair of relative major and minor keys with one less sharp or flat than the original key.

MODULATION

The following keys are closely related to C major:

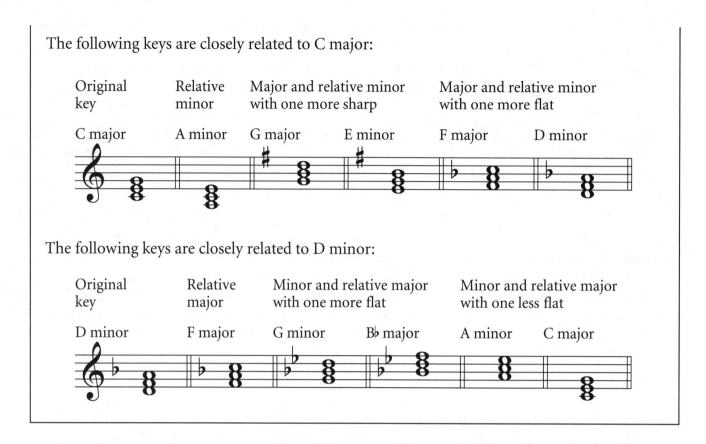

Original key	Relative minor	Major and relative minor with one more sharp		Major and relative minor with one more flat	
C major	A minor	G major	E minor	F major	D minor

The following keys are closely related to D minor:

Original key	Relative major	Minor and relative major with one more flat		Minor and relative major with one less flat	
D minor	F major	G minor	B♭ major	A minor	C major

1. List the closely related keys and write key signatures and the tonic chord for each of the following keys.

C minor

A major

F♯ minor

Db major

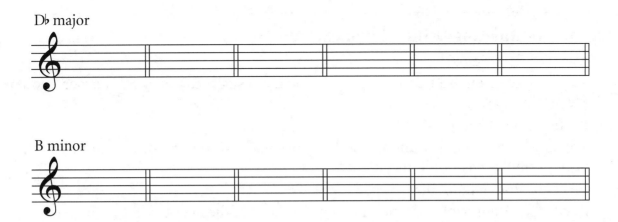

B minor

Modulation Using a Pivot Chord

Modulation to closely related keys is a common feature of 18th-century music. The most common modulation for a major key is to its dominant. For a minor key the most common modulation is to its relative major. These are considered **traditional** or **standard goal keys.**

Closely related keys have one or more chords that are common to both keys. For example, the keys of G and D major both contain the G major triad. Depending on the context, this chord could be analyzed as I in G major or IV in D major. The D minor triad is common to both C major and A minor. This triad could be analyzed as ii in C major or iv in A minor. A **pivot chord** is a chord that is found in both the original key and the key to which the music is modulating (the new key). Pivot chords help to make a modulation smoother.

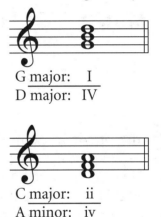

G major: I
D major: IV

C major: ii
A minor: iv

---

1. Provide a harmonic analysis using functional chord symbols for each chord in the two specified keys.

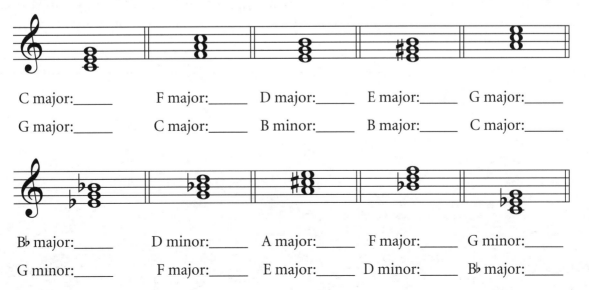

C major:_____   F major:_____   D major:_____   E major:_____   G major:_____

G major:_____   C major:_____   B minor:_____   B major:_____   C major:_____

Bb major:_____   D minor:_____   A major:_____   F major:_____   G minor:_____

G minor:_____   F major:_____   E major:_____   D minor:_____   Bb major:_____

Steps for Modulating Using a Pivot Chord

1. Establish the original key.
   This is done through a harmonic progression that usually contains a V–I progression in the original key.

2. Write the pivot chord.
   This is a chord that is common to both the original and the new key. It must be a tonic or pre-dominant chord in the new key.

3. Write the dominant of the new key.

4. Resolve this dominant to a tonic-functioning chord in the new key (I, I[6], or possibly vi).

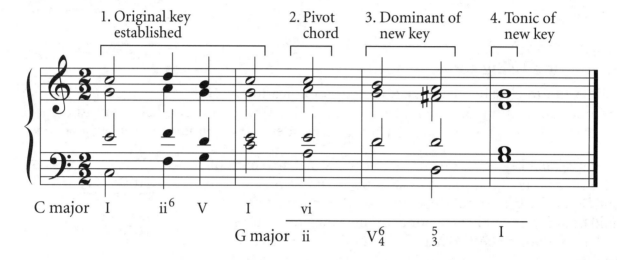

In the previous example, the original key is established with the harmonic progression I–ii[6]–V–I. The perfect cadence firmly establishes the key. The pivot chord functions in both the original and new keys (vi of C major and ii of G major). The dominant area of the new key is decorated with a cadential $\frac{6}{4}$ and resolves to the tonic of the new key. Notice that there is no key-signature change with the modulation. Accidentals are used to reflect the change of key.

In most modulations, the dominant chord is the one that moves the music into the new key. The pivot chord is usually the first chord that precedes the dominant. Because of this, the choice of pivot chord is important. The pivot chord should be a chord that can function as a predominant in the new key. The supertonic or subdominant are good choices. If these are not available, the submediant and tonic in the new key are also effective, but any chord that is common to both keys could work. However, your progression will be stronger if you use chords that have a predominant function.

1. Add functional chord symbols to the following examples, noting the modulation in each.

(a)

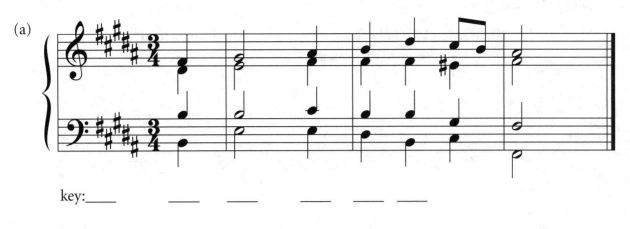

key:____ ____ ____ ____ ____ ____

new key:_____ ____ ____ ____

(b)

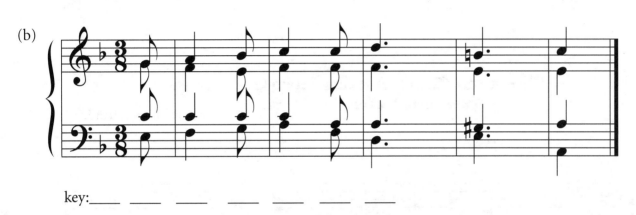

key:____ ____ ____ ____ ____ ____

new key:_____ ____ ____ ____

(c)

key:____ ____ ____ ____ ____ ____

new key:_____ ____ ____ ____ ____

2. Provide a harmonic analysis for the following excerpts using functional and root/quality chord symbols. Identify the pivot chord and symbolize it in both the original and the new key.

Chorale no. 217: Ach Gott, wie manches Herzelied
from **371 Four-Part Chorales**

Johann Sebastian Bach
(1685–1750)

Chorale no. 62: Wer nur den lieben Gott läßt walten
from **371 Four-Part Chorales**

Johann Sebastian Bach
(1685–1750)

Piano Sonata
op. 2, no. 3 (4th movement)

Ludwig van Beethoven
(1770–1827)

3. Complete the following examples for four voices (SATB) according to the given chord symbols.

(a)

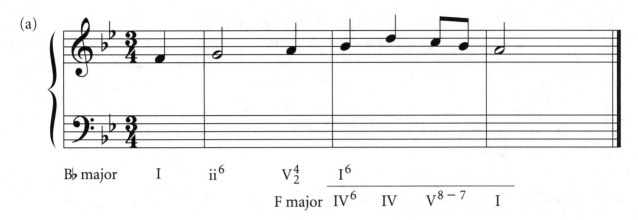

B♭ major   I   ii^6 V$^4_2$ I^6

F major   IV^6 IV   V$^{8-7}$ I

(b)

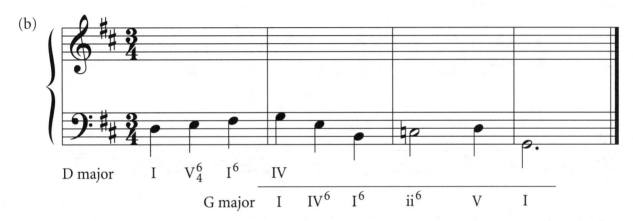

D major   I   V$^6_4$ I^6 IV

G major   I   IV^6 I^6 ii^6 V   I

(c)

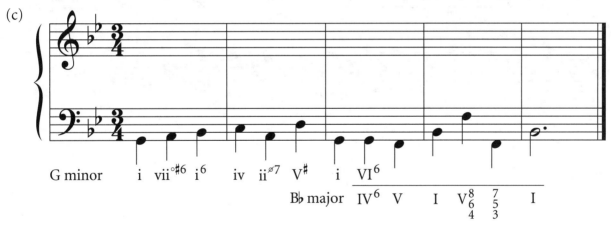

G minor   i   vii$^{°\#6}$ i^6 iv   ii^{ø7} V$^\#$ i   VI^6

B♭ major   IV^6 V   I   V$^8_6{}_4$ $^7_5{}_3$ I

(d)

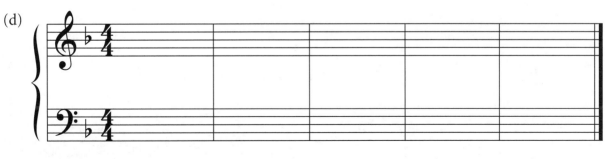

F major   I   VI   ii   V   I   I^6 ii

D minor   iv   V$^\#$ i   V^6 i   VI   iv   V$^6_4$ $^5_\#$ i

4. For the following excerpt, name the key, symbolize the chords with functional chord symbols, and circle and classify any non-chord tones.

Don Ottavio's Aria "Il mio tesoro…"
from **Don Giovanni, act 2**

Wolfgang Amadeus Mozart
(1756–1791)

SUMMARY OF LESSON 26

1. Modulation is a change of key or a shift in tonal center in a composition.

2. The new key is signaled by the prominence of notes or chords that have structural importance in that key. They are either repeated or they form part of a cadence.

3. The majority of modulations will contain accidentals indicating the new key, but this is not always the case. Pieces modulating from minor to relative major may not contain accidentals.

4. A composition may modulate to a closely related key. Two keys are closely related if their key signatures have a difference of no more than one sharp or one flat.

5. There are five closely related keys to any major or minor key:

    • The relative major or minor of the original key.

    • The pair of relative major and minor keys with one more sharp or flat than the original key.

    • The pair of relative major and minor keys with one less sharp or flat than the original key.

6. A pivot chord is a chord that is found in both the original key and the key to which the music is modulating (the new key).

7. The pivot chord should be a chord that can function as a predominant in the new key. The supertonic or subdominant are good choices. If these are not available the submediant and tonic in the new key are also effective, but any chord that is common to both keys could work.

THE BACH CHORALES

The early hymn tunes of the German Protestant church are known as "Chorales." Many chorales had their origins in Latin hymns or folk melodies, but some were original compositions. The chorales of the 16th and 17th centuries were usually written in free rhythm, but by the 18th century, they took on definite metrical structures. Many composers made four-part harmonizations of the chorales for singing in church. Some of the greatest chorale settings were written by Johann Sebastian Bach.

Here are some of the most common features of Bach's chorale harmonizations:

1. Most are in $\frac{4}{4}$ time, but a few are in $\frac{3}{4}$ time.

2. The melodies are usually simple, with the notes harmonized on the quarter-note beat. Occasionally, a quarter-note melody has two chords in eighth notes (for example, ii–vii°6).

3. Longer notes may have more than one chord change, or a single chord decorated with non-chord tones.

4. Each phrase ends with a *fermata* at the cadence.

5. Suspensions and other non-chord tones are used for a more active and expressive texture.

6. The melodic shape of each individual line is important.

The following examples show how Bach used non-chord tones and chordal skips to add interest and motion, and to decorate his harmonizations.

Chorale no. 58: Herzlich lieb hab' ich dich, o Herr
from **371 Four-Part Chorales**

Johann Sebastian Bach
(1685–1750)

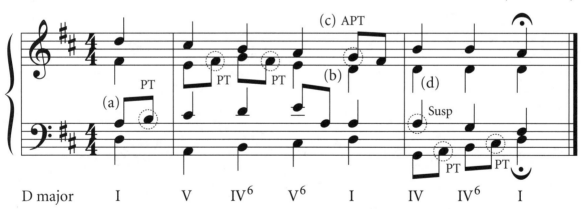

D major   I   V   IV6   V6   I   IV   IV6   I

(a) Unaccented passing tones.

(b) Chordal skips add movement to the harmonization.

(c) Accented passing tones occur frequently.

(d) Suspensions add expressiveness to the texture.

Chorale no. 88: Helft mir Gott's Güte preisen
from 371 Four-Part Chorales

Johann Sebastian Bach
(1685–1750)

A minor V^6 i v^6 vi $ii^{\varnothing6}_5$ V^{8-7} $I^\sharp$

(a) Passing tones may occur in three voices, but they must create logical harmony.

(b) A passing tone is not added in the alto because the leading note should fall a 3rd.

(c) Bach usually wrote chord V first, then added the seventh on a weak beat or weak part of the beat (for example, V^{8-7}).

(d) Often, Bach ended a chorale in a minor key with a tonic major chord. The third of the chord is raised. This ending is called a *tierce de picardie* or picardy third.

Chorale no. 148: Uns ist ein Kindlein heut' gebor'n
from 371 Four-Part Chorales

Johann Sebastian Bach
(1685–1750)

G major

Bach used neighbor tones frequently. They are usually not accented and do not have a strong dissonant effect, but they do add movement to the line. They are often placed between repeated harmony notes, especially when he wants to introduce a more continuous flow.

The most frequently used accented non-chord tones in the Bach chorales are accented passing tones and suspensions. Accented passing tones usually occur in the bass, but can sometimes be found in an inner part. Suspensions occur mainly at cadence points, but can also be found in the middle of phrases.

The texture of chorale writing should be vocal rather than instrumental. Keep within the range of each voice. The use of suspensions is strongly recommended. It is important to check your work for parallel 5ths and octaves, especially when adding non-chord tones. Leaps should not exceed an octave.

If you can obtain a copy of Bach's chorales, play them through and sing the various parts to improve your understanding of how the parts move and fit in with each other, and how they are constructed to suit the voice.

1. Provide a harmonic analysis of the following Bach chorale excerpts using functional chord symbols. Circle and identify any non-chord tones.

Chorale no. 347: Was Gott tut, das ist wohlgetan
from **371 Four-Part Chorales**

(a)

Johann Sebastian Bach
(1685–1750)

key:____

Chorale no. 67: Freu'dich sehr, o meine Seele
from **371 Four-Part Chorales**

(b)

Johann Sebastian Bach
(1685–1750)

key:____

2. Complete the following Bach chorale excerpts by adding the alto and tenor voices.

Chorale no. 293: Was Gott tut, das ist wohlgetan
from **371 Four-Part Chorales**

(a)

Johann Sebastian Bach
(1685–1750)

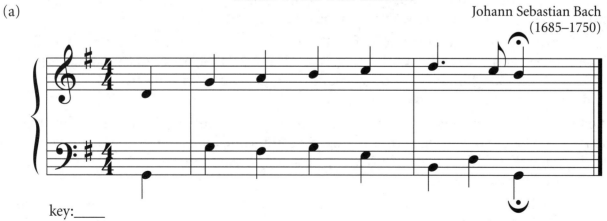

key:____

* NOTE: In Bach's notation, the soprano and alto are written more than an octave apart. Students are reminded that they should not write the soprano and alto more than one octave apart in their own work.

Chorale no. 277: Herzlich lieb hab' ich dich, o Herr
from **371 Four-Part Chorales**

(b)

Johann Sebastian Bach
(1685–1750)

key:____

3. Complete the following phrases from Bach chorales for four voices.

Chorale no. 5: An Wasserflüssen Babylon
from **371 Four-Part Chorales**

(a)

Johann Sebastian Bach
(1685–1750)

key:____

Chorale no. 73: Herr Jesu Christ, du höchstes Gut
from **371 Four-Part Chorales**

(b)

Johann Sebastian Bach
(1685–1750)

key:____

Chorale no. 103: Nun ruhen alle Wälder
from **371 Four-Part Chorales**

(c)

Johann Sebastian Bach
(1685–1750)

key:____

The following excerpt is a fragment from a Bach chorale written in open score with the text. Note that each voice sings the same word or syllable at the same time. Every voice must sing the text. Held or tied notes that result in the omission of a syllable must be avoided. Repeated notes that "stutter" on one syllable of text must also be avoided.

Chorale no. 80: O Haupt voll Blut und Wunden
from **371 Four-Part Chorales**

Johann Sebastian Bach
(1685–1750)

Here is the same excerpt written in short score with the text placed above the staff.

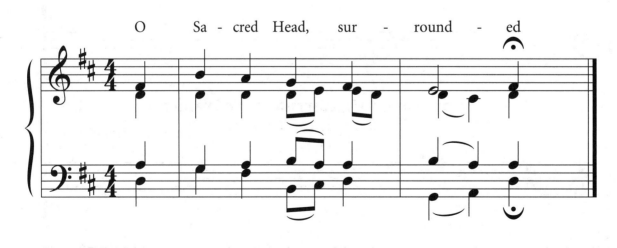

4. Complete the following chorale excerpts for four voices (SATB). Show all functional chord symbols.

Chorale no. 20: Ein' feste Burg ist unser Gott
from **371 Four-Part Chorales**

(a)

Johann Sebastian Bach
(1685–1750)

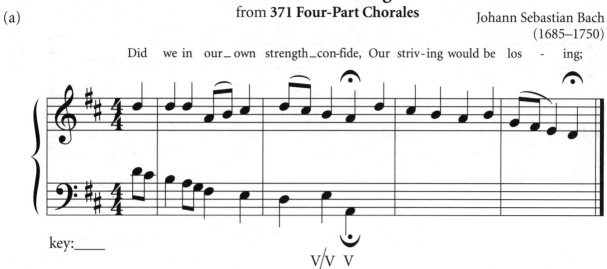

Chorale no. 158: Der Tag, der ist so freudenreich
from **371 Four-Part Chorales**

(b)

Johann Sebastian Bach
(1685–1750)

Chorale no. 128: Alles ist an Gottes Segen
from 371 Four-Part Chorales

(c)

Johann Sebastian Bach
(1685–1750)

Al - les ist an Got - tes Se - gen

key:____

Chorale no. 72: Erhalt'uns, Herr, bei deinem Wort
from 371 Four-Part Chorales

(d)

Johann Sebastian Bach
(1685–1750)

Er - halt uns,— Herr bei— dei - nem Wort,

key:____

Chorale no. 309: Ein Lämmlein geht und trägt die Schuld
from 371 Four-Part Chorales

(e)

Johann Sebastian Bach
(1685–1750)

Him - self with— pa - tience He— pre - pares. To

key:____

die for ev - ery— na - tion

Lesson 28
Form and Analysis

You will be studying and analyzing the dance movements from various periods. Dance suites were written in Western Europe from approximately 1650 to 1750 by many leading composers, such as Johann Sebastian Bach, François Couperin, Henry Purcell, George Frideric Handel, and Johann Jakob Froberger. Each dance form has certain characteristics that you should be aware of. The following chart provides a summary of the styles, characteristics, and tempos of these dances. These characteristics also apply to dances from the Classical and later periods.

Allemande *Almain* *Allmayne* *Alamand*	Time signature:	$\frac{4}{4}$ or $\frac{2}{2}$
	Italian marking:	*Allegretto, Moderato, Allegro moderato*
	Characteristics:	one-note upbeat (usually one sixteenth note); often a flow of continuous running sixteenth notes throughout
Courante *Corrente*	Time signature:	$\frac{3}{4}$, $\frac{3}{2}$, $\frac{3}{8}$, or $\frac{6}{4}$
	Italian marking:	*Allegro, Vivace* (Italian *Corrente*), *Moderato* (French *Courante*)
	Characteristics:	light texture and rapid figures (means "running"); Italian *corrente* is in quick triple time (usually $\frac{3}{4}$) with running passages; French *courante* is in a moderate tempo (in $\frac{3}{2}$ or $\frac{6}{4}$) with shifts from triple to duple time (*hemiola*)
Bourrée *Borry*	Time signature:	$\frac{2}{4}$ or $\frac{4}{4}$ or $\frac{2}{2}$
	Italian marking:	*Vivace, Allegro Vivace*
	Characteristics:	French dance; quarter-note (or two eighth-note) upbeat; quick duple time; rhythmic and bright with steady quarter notes
Sarabande	Time signature:	$\frac{3}{2}$ or $\frac{3}{4}$
	Italian marking:	*Adagio, Lento*
	Characteristics:	Spanish dance; chordal in texture; usually no upbeat; often prolonged or accented note on second beat
Minuet *Minuetto* *Menuet* *Menuetto*	Time signature:	$\frac{3}{4}$ or $\frac{3}{8}$
	Italian marking:	*Moderato grazioso, Andante*
	Characteristics:	French dance; unhurried tempo; graceful

Gigue *Giga*	Time signature:	$\frac{6}{8}$ or simple time in triplets
	Italian marking:	*Allegro, Vivace, Presto*
	Characteristics:	derived from the English word jig, but evolved differently in Italy and France: French *gigue* is in compound time (often $\frac{6}{8}$) with polyphonic texture; Italian *giga* is faster than French *gigue* and has running notes, usually over chordal harmony
Gavotte	Time signature:	$\frac{4}{4}$ or $\frac{2}{2}$
	Italian marking:	*Allegro, Allegro moderato*
	Characteristics:	French dance; usually two quarter-note upbeats, so the phrase begins and ends in the middle of the measure
March	Time signature:	$\frac{4}{4}$
	Italian marking:	*Alla marcia, Allegro marziale*
	Characteristics:	sometimes quarter-note upbeat; military origins
Passepied	Time signature:	$\frac{3}{4}$, $\frac{3}{2}$, or $\frac{3}{8}$
	Italian marking:	*Allegro*
	Characteristics:	French dance; occasionally one-note upbeat; rapid dance
Rigaudon *Rigadoon*	Time signature:	$\frac{2}{2}$ or $\frac{4}{4}$
	Italian marking:	*Vivace, Allegro Vivace*
	Characteristics:	French dance; quarter-note upbeat; rhythmic and bright
Polonaise	Time signature:	$\frac{3}{4}$
	Italian marking:	*Moderato, Allegro moderato*
	Characteristics:	stately Polish dance in triple meter; no upbeat; often short repeated rhythmic motive
Siciliano *Sicilienne*	Time signature:	$\frac{6}{8}$ or $\frac{12}{8}$
	Italian marking:	*Andante, Andantino*
	Characteristics:	Italian dance originated in Sicily; usually compound duple time but can be compound quadruple; swaying rhythm; often in a minor key

1. Name the dance type for each of the following excerpts from suites by Johann Sebastian Bach. Give an appropriate tempo marking for each.

French Suite no. 5 in G major
BWV 816

(a) Tempo:_____

Johann Sebastian Bach
(1685–1750)

dance type:_____

Partita no. 1 in B flat major
BWV 825

(b) Tempo:_____

Johann Sebastian Bach
(1685–1750)

dance type:_____

Partita no. 1 in B flat major
BWV 825

(c) Tempo:_____

Johann Sebastian Bach
(1685–1750)

dance type:_____

French Suite no. 4 in E flat major
BWV 815

(d) Tempo:_____

Johann Sebastian Bach
(1685–1750)

dance type:_____

French Suite no. 3 in B minor
BWV 814

(e) Tempo:_____

Johann Sebastian Bach
(1685–1750)

dance type:_____

French Suite no. 6 in E major
BWV 817

(f) Tempo:_____

Johann Sebastian Bach
(1685–1750)

dance type:_____

Binary Form

Binary form is a two-part form. Usually, each of the two sections is repeated, but not always. Label the first section with the letter **A** and the second section with the letter **B**.

There are three types of binary form:

> Symmetrical binary form
> Asymmetrical binary form
> Rounded binary form

In binary form, the two sections are often contrasting in character. If A and B are the same length (the same number of measures), the form is called **symmetrical binary**. If A and B are different lengths, the form is called **asymmetrical binary**. In this case, B is usually longer than A.

Section A starts in the tonic key. It may end with a perfect cadence in the dominant key. It may end with a perfect or an imperfect cadence in the tonic key. If the piece is in a minor key, section A may cadence in the tonic key, or it may modulate to the relative major or to the dominant, ending with a perfect cadence in the new key. Section A is usually grouped in four-measure phrases, but not always. Occasionally, other phrase lengths may occur.

Section B may start in the key that section A ended in, or it may begin in the tonic key. This section may modulate to a closely related key, but it modulates back to the tonic key to end with a perfect cadence. Section B is usually grouped in four-measure phrases, but irregular phrase lengths sometimes occur.

The following *Bourrée* is in symmetrical binary form. Section A is eight measures long and section B is eight measures long. Section A ends with a perfect cadence in the dominant (F major). Section B returns to the tonic (B flat major) at the end. Phrases are marked. The large letters placed on the score indicate the sections. A tempo indication is given, and the key and type of each cadence are identified at the ends of phrases.

Bourrée in B flat major

Form: Symmetrical binary
Tempo: Allegro

Johann Pachelbel
(1653–1706)

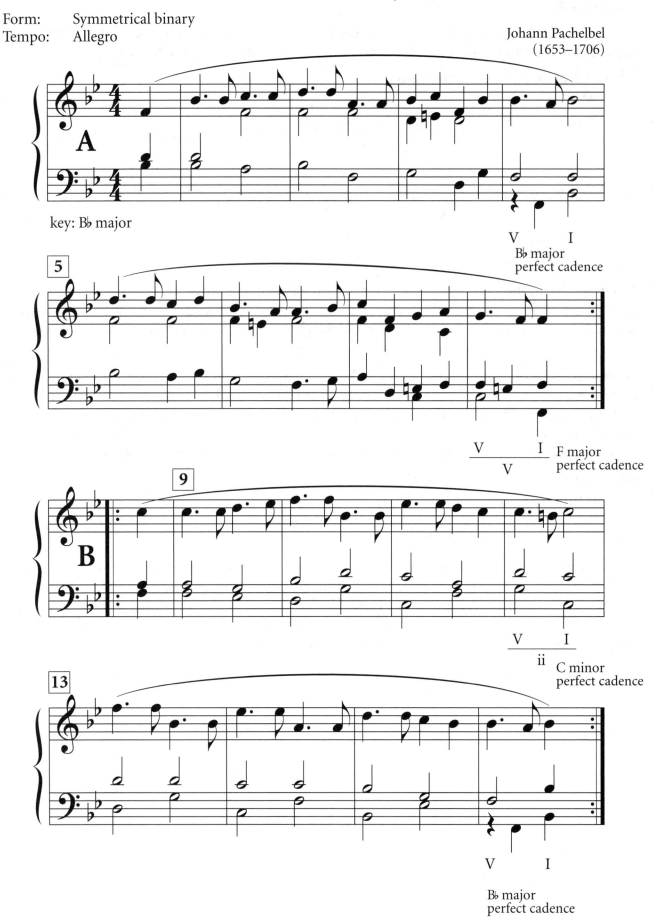

Rounded Binary Form

In **rounded binary** form, section A returns at the end of the B section and is included in the section repeat signs.

Section A¹ starts in the tonic key. It may end with a perfect cadence in the dominant. It may also end with a perfect cadence (if repeat signs are used) or an imperfect cadence in the tonic. If the piece is in a minor key, section A¹ may cadence in the tonic key or modulate to the relative major, or to the dominant, and cadence in the new key. This section is usually grouped in four-measure phrases.

Section B usually begins in the key in which A¹ ended. Section B may modulate to closely related keys. It may end with a perfect cadence in a related key, or it may end in the key in which it started.

Section A² may begin exactly like A¹, or it may be a slightly different variation of A¹. There may only be a partial restatement of A¹, or it may be in a different voice or octave. The beginning of A² must be recognizable and in the tonic key. A transposition of A¹ to another key does not constitute a recapitulation of A. This section ends with a perfect cadence in the tonic key.

Note that Section A¹ is repeated, and then B and A² are repeated together.

If there are no repeat signs, the cadence at the end of A¹ determines whether the form is rounded binary or ternary. If this cadence is open (imperfect in key I, or any cadence in another key), the form is rounded binary. If the cadence is closed (perfect in I), the form is ternary.

The *Minuet* on the following page is in rounded binary form. Section A¹ is eight measures long, section B is eight measures long, and A² is eight measures also.

Section A¹ ends with an open (imperfect) cadence in the tonic key (F major). The first phrase of section B cadences in ii (G minor) and moves back to the tonic key. A² is a restatement of A¹ with the first phrase ending on a deceptive cadence, and the final phrase cadencing in the home key of F major. Section A¹ is repeated, and B and A² are repeated together.

Minuet in F major
K 2

Form: Rounded binary
Tempo: Moderato

Wolfgang Amadeus Mozart
(1756–1791)

Ternary Form

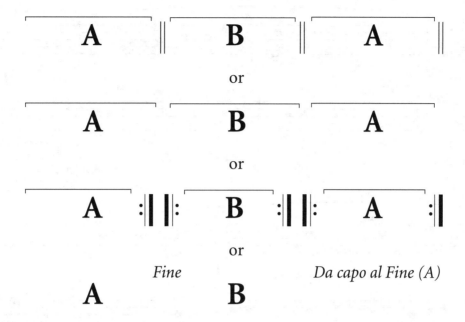

or

or

Fine   *Da capo al Fine (A)*

or

A   B

Ternary form is a three-part form.

Section A is usually grouped in four-measure phrases. Section A always starts in the tonic key and ends with a perfect cadence in the tonic key.

Section B is often contrasted, in character and in themes, to section A. Frequently, it is in a closely related key to section A. It may end with a cadence in a new key, or it may end with a cadence in the tonic key.

The final **Section A** is a repeat of the original section A, but it can be slightly varied. This section may be written out, or it may be indicated by the marking *D.C. al Fine.*

The *Bourrée* on the following page is in ternary form. Each section is four measures long. Section A cadences in a perfect closed cadence in A minor. Section B moves into and cadences in the relative major (C major). Section A is restated and cadences in a perfect closed cadence in the tonic key.

Bourrée in A minor

Form: Ternary
Tempo: Allegro

Johann Krieger
(1652–1735)

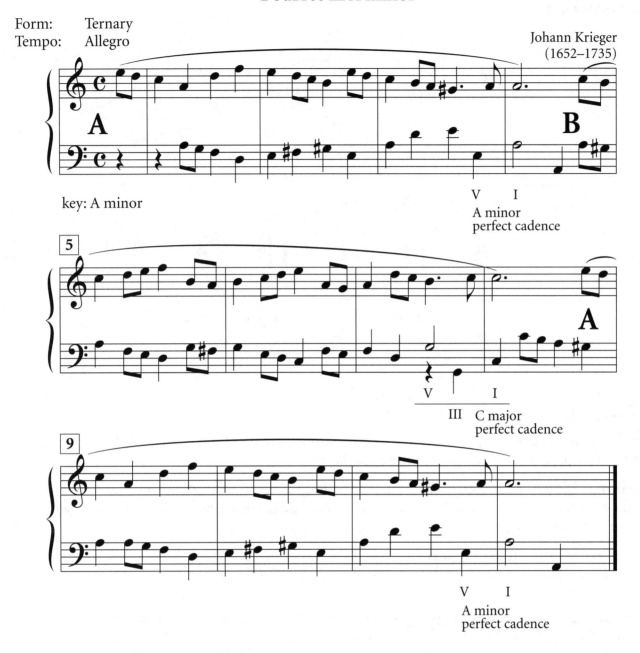

Remember that dances in ternary form can use *D.C. al Fine* in place of a written-out repeat of the A section.

Modulation in Baroque Dances

Baroque dance movements almost always change key and when they do, it is common to modulate to a traditional or standard goal key. The traditional goal key for a dance in a major key is the dominant, and for a minor key, the relative major or dominant minor.

These pieces will only modulate to a closely related key. Since these dances may only contain two voices, it can be difficult to determine where the key change occurs and what the new key is. The easiest way to recognize some of these key changes is to look for the presence of accidentals that are not part of the key signature. A raised note may be the leading note of a new key. For example, if a piece in F major modulates to its dominant, you will probably see B naturals indicating the new key of C major. However, notes altered by accidentals may also appear as chromatic non-chord tones or secondary dominants and not reflect a key change. Occasionally, especially in a piece with only two voices, a key change may occur without the use of accidentals in the music. In this case the accidentals may be implied.

When a minor-key piece modulates to its relative major, it may not require accidentals since the two keys share the same key signature. In this case, examine the bass line at the end of the phrase. A perfect cadence is usually supported by $\hat{5}$–$\hat{1}$ in the bass. Look at the bass notes and determine if they indicate a perfect cadence in the original key or a new key. Check the other voice or voices to see if they contain the notes to provide the correct harmony for a perfect cadence.

FORM AND ANALYSIS

1. For each of the following dances, mark the phrasing, name the key, and add functional chord symbols at the cadence points. Name the cadences, identify the form, and identify the sections with letters placed directly on the score. Choose an appropriate tempo.

(a)
Borry [Saraband] in D major
D 219/2

Form: _____

Tempo: _____

attr. to Henry Purcell
(*ca* 1659–1695)

key:____

(b)

Form: _____

Tempo: _____

Minuetto
from **Sonatina in G major**

Thomas Attwood
(1765–1838)

Source: *Easy Progressive Lessons Fingered for Young Beginners on the Pianoforte or Harpsichord, ca* 1795

FORM AND ANALYSIS

(c)

Sarabande
from **Violin Sonata, op. 5, no. 7 (3rd movement)**

Form: _____

Tempo: _____

Arcangelo Corelli
(1653–1713)

(i) Give the measure numbers for a phrase based on a descending stepwise bass line. _____

(ii) Provide the root/quality symbol for the chord in m. 6. _____

(iii) Why is the leading note not raised in m. 6? _____

(iv) Give the measure numbers for a phrase based on a descending 5ths sequence.

_____

(d)

Bourrée

Form: _____

Tempo: _____

Johann Sebastian Bach
(1685–1750)

key:____

Source: *Partita in B minor for Solo Violin*, BWV 1002

(i)   Find the passage based on the chord symbols A7–Dm–G7–C. Write these symbols directly on the score where the passage occurs. Name the type of sequence created by these chords. _____

(e)

Menuet
from the Notebook for Wolfgang

Form: _____

Tempo: _____

attr. to Leopold Mozart
(1719–1787)

key:_____

(i) Circle the right-hand part in m. 2. Circle all other occurrences of this motive throughout this piece, including transpositions.

(f)

Minuet in G minor

Form: _____

Tempo: _____

Gottfried Heinrich Stölzel
(1690–1749)

key:_____

Source: *Clavierbüchlein vor Wilhelm Friedemann Bach*

(i) Name the key and provide functional chord symbols for mm. 13–20.

(ii) Does this piece modulate to a traditional goal key? _____

(g)

Gigue à l'anglaise
from **Partita in G major, TWV 32:1**

Form: _____

Tempo: _____

Georg Philipp Telemann
(1681–1767)

key:_____

(i) Octave doubling occurs in mm. 8 and 16. What "rule" of traditional harmony and counterpoint is broken here?_____

(h)

A March
(Taylor 433)

Form: _____

Tempo: _____

Jeremiah Clarke
(*ca* 1674–1707)

key:_____

(i)

Minuet in A minor
Z 649

Form: _____

Tempo: _____

Henry Purcell
(*ca* 1659–1695)

key: _____

(i)   Find a phrase with a descending stepwise bass line.

(ii) Provide the root/quality chord symbols for that phrase.

(iii) Label the type of cadence that occurs in mm. 11–12.

(j)

Waltz in A major
from **Erste Walzer, D 365**

Form: _____

Tempo: _____

Franz Schubert
(1797–1828)

key:_____

(i) Circle the right-hand part in m. 1. Circle all other occurrences of this motive and above it, briefly describe how it is varied in each case.

(ii) Find and circle the applied or secondary dominants in this piece.

(iii) Label the neighboring $^6_4$ chord directly on the score.

(k)

Rigadoon in A minor

Form: _____

Tempo: _____

William Babell
(1690–1723)

key:_____

(i)   Circle the statement that best describes the opening of this piece:
   (a) SATB texture
   (b) imitation at the unison
   (c) two-part imitation at the octave, one beat later
   (d) inversion of the opening motive.

(ii) Give the measure numbers of three places where this statement occurs
      again._____

(iii) Provide the root/quality chord symbol for the chord at the end of this piece.

(iv) What is the name for this kind of ending? _____

(1)

Bourrée anglaise
from Sonata in G major for Flute and Basso Continuo, HWV 363b

Form: _____

Tempo: _____

George Frideric Handel
(1685–1759)

key:_____

(i) Find and label a chain of suspensions over a descending 5ths progression.

(ii) Find and circle all examples of a syncopated rhythmic motive.

Lesson 29
Melody Writing 2

Sixteen-Measure Melodies

One of the strongest techniques for developing a melody is repetition. Repetition of a melody or motive is a basic means of formal growth. The following is the melody introduced in Lesson 23. Beethoven repeats the same melodic idea for phrases 1, 2, and 4 and varies them through his use of cadences. Phrase 3 provides contrast. This phrase begins in the same way as the earlier phrases, but on a different tonal level. After the first three notes, the melody changes direction, introduces eighth-note motion, and ends with a secondary dominant. This change provides balance and contrast both melodically and harmonically. Beethoven completes the melody by repeating the opening material and ending with a perfect closed cadence.

Symphony no. 9 in D minor
(4th movement)

Ludwig van Beethoven
(1770–1827)

In this lesson we will extend a given melodic opening and create a sixteen-measure composition with four four-measure phrases. The style of this melody will be that of an 18th-century dance in rounded binary form using repeat signs.

Consider these questions as they relate to the following example:

1. Name the type of Baroque dance that it represents.

2. Name the key.

3. Mark the structural phrasing

4. Indicate the implied harmony using functional chord symbols.

5. Complete the upper voice to create a melodic composition in rounded binary form. The complete composition will have four four-measure phrases, for a total of sixteen measures. Use repeat signs appropriate to the form.

6. In mm. 9–16, add a bass part at the cadences only. Complete the unused portion of the bass staff with rests.

7. At each of the cadences, write functional chord symbols and name the type of cadence.

Dance type:_____

Key:_____

Step 1: Analyze the Given Melody

- To determine the type of Baroque dance, look at the time signature and tempo and if the melody begins with an upbeat. This melody is in $\frac{6}{8}$ time with the tempo marking of Allegro. There is no upbeat. Using this information we can determine that the dance type is a gigue.

- The key is F major.

- As in most Baroque dances, the melody falls into two four-measure phrases. These are marked directly on the score.

- The harmony implied at the end of the first phrase forms an imperfect cadence with a cadential $\frac{6}{4}$. The harmony at the end of the second phrase implies a perfect cadence with a cadential $\frac{6}{4}$. Functional chord symbols are added indicating the implied harmony and the cadences are named as imperfect and perfect.

- The melody remains in the tonic and does not modulate. The melodies in this question will not involve modulation and will remain in the tonic key throughout.

- The second phrase begins with a repetition of the first phrase but the ending of this phrase is changed. The melody ends on $\hat{2}$–$\hat{1}$, which allows for a perfect closed cadence.

Dance type: Gigue

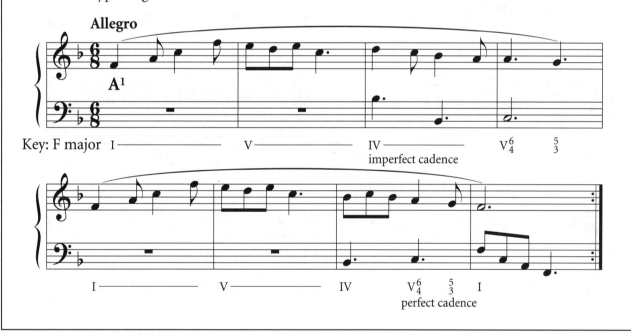

Step 2: Lay Out the New Melody

Divide the staff into two four-measure phrases and add repeat signs. It is very important to place all of the notational elements in the correct place. In the example below, notice where the repeat signs and the key signature are placed. Measure numbers are not necessary, but can be helpful.

Dance type: Gigue

Step 3: Write Out Phrase 4

Since this melody will be in rounded binary form, the A section must return at the end. Measures 5–8 begin with a repeat of the opening melodic idea, but end with a perfect closed cadence. The next step is to rewrite mm. 5–8 in mm. 13–16. Since mm. 5–8 ended with a perfect closed cadence in the tonic key, you may copy them exactly as they originally appeared. This step is essential to creating a melody in rounded binary form. Note that the repeat signs are also necessary here: since **A**[1] ends with a perfect closed cadence in the tonic key, the repeat signs are required to create rounded binary form.

Step 4: Write Out Phrase 3

This phrase should maintain the style of the dance, but should offer some contrast to the material already given. Composition involves repetition and contrast. Since we have used the element of repetition already, this phrase will provide much-needed contrast. The phrase should be in the tonic key and end with an imperfect cadence. Remember to try and maintain some of the rhythmic elements used in the previous material. Introducing new or dramatically different rhythmic figures from those already seen may make this phrase too contrasting and it may sound like it does not belong with the piece. You may want to take a previously used rhythmic fragment and vary it melodically.

In the example below, mm. 9–10 are an inversion of m. 1. Measures 11–12 contain an imperfect cadence in the tonic. The left-hand figure from m. 8 is used here for cadential unity and helps the motion of the dance continue. Make sure that your melody makes harmonic sense. The melody should imply a logical harmonic progression.

Dance type: Gigue

Study the following example of a minor-key melody with an upbeat.

The key of this melody remains in E minor throughout. The first phrase ends with an imperfect cadence. The second phrase begins with a repetition of the first phrase but the ending is altered to accommodate a perfect cadence. The phrases are four measures long and each one begins with a two-note upbeat. The B section begins with a two note upbeat and the melody, although related rhythmically to the previous material, is different melodically. This provides contrast to the melody in the A section. The B section is four measures long and ends with an imperfect cadence in the tonic. Since this is rounded binary form, the A section returns for the last phrase and concludes the piece with a perfect cadence in the tonic. Repeat signs are used to maintain the rounded binary form.

Study the placement of the repeat signs, rests, key signature, time signature, and upbeat notes. It is important to use the correct notation when writing these melodies. Also note the use of accidentals for the key of E minor and the perfect closed cadences ending on $\hat{7}$–$\hat{1}$.

Dance type: Gavotte

Key: E minor

MELODY WRITING 2

For each of the following melodies:

1. Name the type of Baroque dance that it represents.
2. Name the key.
3. Mark the structural phrasing
4. Indicate the implied harmony using functional and root/quality chord symbols.
5. Complete the upper voice to create a melodic composition in rounded binary form. The complete composition will have four four-measure phrases, for a total of sixteen measures. Use repeat signs appropriate to the form.
6. In mm. 9–16, add a bass part at the cadences only. Complete the unused portion of the bass staff with rests.
7. At each of the cadences, write functional chord symbols and name the type of cadence.

(a)   Dance type:_____

Key:_____

(b)   Dance type:_____

Key:_____

Melody Writing 2

(c)   Dance type:_____

Key:_____

(d)   Dance type:_____

Allegretto

Key:_____

MELODY WRITING 2

(e)   Dance type:_____

Key:_____

(f)   Dance type:_____

Allegro marziale

Key:_____

Melody Writing 2

(g)   Dance type:_____

Key:_____

Terms

SOURCES FOR MUSIC EXAMPLES